Apart, I Am Together

Apart, I Am Together

For Debbie and Nils,
fellow travelers and seekers
of truth. Tom Donlon
5/21/23

TOM DONLON

RESOURCE *Publications* • Eugene, Oregon

APART, I AM TOGETHER

Resource Publications
An Imprint of Wipf and Stock Publishers
199 W. 8th Ave., Suite 3
Eugene, OR 97401

www.wipfandstock.com

PAPERBACK ISBN: 978-1-6667-6670-7
HARDCOVER ISBN: 978-1-6667-6671-4
EBOOK ISBN: 978-1-6667-6672-1

02/08/23

To Beth Wife and the Sweebs

CONTENTS

Contents

Contents

CONTENTS

ACKNOWLEDGMENTS

The following poems were published in these journals, newspapers, anthologies and in the thirty-poem chapbook *Peregrine*, published by Franciscan University, Steubenville, Ohio, in 2016:

ABZ (and *Peregrine*): "Skull"

AHA (Jefferson County Arts Newsletter; and *Peregrine*): "Ghazal for Jitterbug"

America (and *Peregrine*): "Baby"

Anthology of Appalachian Writers, Barbara Kingsolver Volume 15 (Shepherd University): "Thirty-Nine Cicada Wings" and "Death Row Interview"

Antietam Review (first two also in *Peregrine*): "An Anglo-Saxon Unwittingly Supports the Teleological Argument for Design," "Ryan's Chair," and "Lucy and Lily"

Blue Collar Review (also reprinted in the 2009 anthology *Appalachia's Last Stand* and in *Peregrine*): "Sago"

Chest Journal: "Chest Pains"

Christianity and Literature: "Abishag"

Commonweal (and *Peregrine*): "To St. Peter"

Fluent (and *Peregrine*): "An Iraqi Soldier" and "Staunton-Parkersburg Turnpike"

Folio (first one also in *Peregrine*): "Headless Barbies" and "Stones"

Form Quarterly: "Why I Like the Villanelle"

Good News Paper, Shepherdstown, WV (second and seventh also in *Peregrine*): "A Bricklayer's Helper," "Ballet Lesson," "Burning Bush," "Hymn to My Wife Doing Laundry," "Jealousy and Envy," "Love Poem," "Spring Concert at the Middle School," and "White Birch in Winter"

Harpers Ferry Community Newsletter: "Viola"

Hospital Drive: "New Terms"

Idioms: "Troweling"

In Good Company: Poets Celebrate Shepherdstown's 250th Anniversary (third one originally in *ABZ*; second and third also in *Peregrine*): "Driving Range," "Junction," and "Skull"

International Journal of Healthcare & Humanities (Penn State): "Fibroadenoma"

In the Midst—A COVID-19 Anthology: "Toilet Paper"

Kestrel: "In Walmart after Being Published in the Local Paper" and "Rejection Slip"

The Messenger (a publication of American University's MFA program): "Popindoo Hat Man"

Northern Appalachia Review: "Hornet Nest" and "Square Knots"

The Observer, Shepherdstown, WV: "Cypress Trees"

ACKNOWLEDGMENTS

ONLY THE SEA KEEPS: Poetry of the Tsunami (also in *Peregrine*): "Tsunami"

Pensive (Northeastern University): "Unity," "Red-Winged Blackbird," and "Frankensteina"

Peregrine (poems originally published in chapbook): "Peregrine," "During a Sermon, I Think of Einstein's Theory on the Speed of Gravity," "Ex Cathedra," "Explaining Santa," "Hairdo," "I Do," and "Mia Rose at Four"

Poet Lore: "Saipan" and "Junk Drawers"

Poetry: Works on Walls 2011: "Bluebirds"

Poetry X Hunger: "Yes, They Were Hungry"

Ridgeways: "Apart, I Am Together"

Shepherdstown Chronicle: The following poems were published as part of the Bookend Poets' column: "A Blind Man in Autumn," "B-17 over Berlin," "Beer Cans," "Bird Feeder, Bird Bath," "Blueberry Pie" (also in *Peregrine*), "Bottle Collecting," "Cleaning the Range Top" (also in *Peregrine*), "Cod Fisher" (also in *Peregrine*), "Dylan Takes the Floor" (also in *Peregrine*), "Fishing," "For the Memory of Greg Bender," "Grass," "Interpreting Blurs," "Lighthouse," "Maple Syruping," "Math Homework," "Men on Mowers—Early Fall," "No One in Particular," "Paintings" (also in *Peregrine*), "Perfume," "Rush Hour and a Half" (and in *Peregrine*), "Slug," "Snapping Turtle," "Speed Boating at Dam 4," "Sunset on Blue Ridge" (also in *Peregrine*), "Troweling," "Tulips at Easter" (also in *Peregrine*), and "Vocabulary"

The Appalachian Compilation (anthology produced by the Mountain Scribes, 2018): "Mulching the Rock Garden" and "October Hike with Copperhead"

The Rolling Coulter: "Ode to Man with Backhoe"

The Sow's Ear Poetry Review: "Parallel Parking in December" (also in *Peregrine*) and "Rice"

WILD SWEET NOTES II: An Anthology of WV Poets (both also in *Peregrine*): "Ryan's Chair" and "Blueberry Pie"

RUSH HOUR AND A HALF

You make this run five days a week,
the office sixty miles from the country.
You slalom at dawn down the Blue Ridge
one car in a string of pearls down Route 9
to where the work is—down a two-lane,
tree-lined, state maintained—oh never the same
since you hit a deer, every glimmer doe eyes,
every mailbox a buck. You sip coffee,
scan soy bean fields, listen to books on CD.

Out of the woods, you merge, soft-pedal
for a place on the by-pass, stiffen.
The guy next to you is shaving.
Everyone passes the school bus,
the road grader. Close to the city
pace slows, crawls. Toll road. You merge,
each car in turn, as a zipper closing.
Here you are sitting still. A lady powders.
A man reads the news. Someone enjoys a bagel.

On the roadside, gems glitter:
shards of headlight, clusters of rubies, diamonds,
shimmering chrome. Bumper stickers:
"One more dopeless hope fiend," says one,
"Live right, eat well, die anyway," another.
We are in this together solving clues
on personalized license plates. We quietly drive,
stay between the lines, swerve when we must,
follow this road because we know no other.

AN ANGLO-SAXON UNWITTINGLY SUPPORTS THE TELEOLOGICAL ARGUMENT FOR DESIGN

Daylight fills the furrows of our plowed earth,
and I beseech the Lamb to bless me as I work
the fields, milk the cows as hogs and chickens sing
their barnyard songs. The house is still as death,
yet the fair wife, heavy with child, makes a low laugh,
gives a full breast to our bright son new to life.

We give thanks each day and look to heaven for life,
for we're but a breath from turning back to earth.
As wealth turns to woe and woe to wealth I laugh
and am glad to put my sweaty hands to work
to plow the fields, to shut the door to death,
to eat and drink, to pound my chest, and sing.

When thunder clouds bring rain for crops, I sing
of yellow fields, of plums and pears and, yes, of life.
To grow, the seed must go the way of death.
Its green, blind eye must know the rot of earth
to find its roots, to stretch its legs, to work
its arms above the ground, to clap its hands and laugh.

In the blowing wind, I plant the wheat and laugh.
In the drench of rain, I roar and hear my heart sing
of the newborn giving suck, of seed at work
in the womb of my good wife. May our years of life
bring only harvest in the deep trough of this earth.
Keep us from the pit of hell. Take us softly to death.

Our souls, at times, have feared the black of death.
We go cold to the bone, hold our brows, but laugh
and cling with hope to the light that cradles the earth
after even the darkest, starless night. The sparrows sing,
the finches build their nests, hatch their broods, bring life
to the farm and find a place in the heave of its work.

Yoked, my wife and I plow our way and work
through drought and storm and tire nearly to death.
Under a roof with fire in the hearth, we make a life.
Arm in arm and in the bed we kiss and laugh.
With my sword beaten to a plowshare, I sing
a truce with men and delve the clay of this red earth.

Work hard, bow the knee, let mirth fill your days on earth.
Love the wife, climb the hills of your hilly life, and sing.
When time to give up the ghost, laugh in the mouth of death.

SKULL

Jawless, it rolled from an earth pile after rain
at the elementary school construction site.
Workers, laying pipe, thought it was a rock.
Work stopped. Police wrapped the area with tape.

The graded ground covers sinew and bone, synapse
and cell. An African American girl, pre-Civil War,
lost her lowest denominator. Even when my Lab died,
I curled her paws in rest before I shoveled earth on her.

The tape is gone. Sewer pipe is in. Grass grows.
Skeletal frames of scaffolding aid masons
who lay block for walls. Soon, a curving road
will sing with busloads of children packed for school.

She seeks her parts: breast bone, widening pelvis,
and someone to tell what left her there alone and apart.
You will hear, young one, bursts of laughter, children
on swings, their ears open to hear a field that speaks.

TSUNAMI

the
syllables
smooth smooth
as water swish through
the wind of your mouth roll
out like a wave tsunami tsunami
tsu tsu tsu you purse your lips blow
out the name tsu tsu tsu soothing smooth
say it slowly na na na the crest rises rises rises
hauls back the coastal waters whoosh pulls off the clothes
of the shoreline comes in fast fast and low low too fast
to see to see hello hello mi mi mi the receding
receding into the mouth of its leaving its leaving
oh the delirious inconsolable grieving grieving
the muddy littoral the littoral is leaving
goodbye goodbye goodbye into the deep
the deep oblivious blue sea the sea
villages and towns are missing
tsunami tsunami tsunami
where can the missing
ones be the little
ones the little
ones

APART, I AM TOGETHER

I always had opinions for my mother
to counter hers for me. As the first son,
I thought she should tell her daughter
what to do. I didn't know that, as a wife,
she was acting on behalf of her husband,
the man who doubled as my father.

It's a time-tried idea, a father
living with a woman who is mother
to their children. The role of husband
is old enough, but new when a son
sets his mind to having a wife.
What he'll find is someone's daughter.

My oldest sister, the first daughter,
held a special place with my father,
but not so special as that of his wife.
I shared him with siblings and mother,
but my affections were from a son
not knowing the part of a husband.

That was childhood. As a husband,
I'm married to another's daughter,
but she has left her parents as this son
has broken from the house of father
and from the arms of mother.
Apart, I am together with my wife,

or at least she is becoming a wife,
as I am learning the part of husband.
She reflects upon her mother
who lost to marriage her first daughter
as I consider the life of my father
who lost to marriage his oldest son.

He knows, though, he hasn't lost a son:
as I try to be a man for my wife,
I copy what I learned from my father,
things that make me like him, a husband.
And my wife, the one-time daughter,
finds she is going to be a mother.

Imagine having a son, this young husband,
or my wife giving birth to a daughter.
How soon we have become as father and mother.

THE WOMAN AT JACOB'S WELL

He sat on the edge of the well
weary, I suppose, from some journey.
His feet were caked with dust.
He asked me to draw a cup
for him from my water pot.

I could not understand,
of course, why he would ask me,
a Samaritan. When I asked him,
he said he would give a drink
to me. But he had no cup,
so I thought him to be at riddles.

Living water, he said, flowing
from me. Ignore him, I thought.
He has traveled.

Parched lips told me
those who drink from Jacob's well
will thirst again. What could I do
but ask him for this wellspring
of living water? But he mocked me.

Get my husband, he said,
when he knew I had none.
Strange. He knew me. He told me
everything I have ever done.

In my haste, I left my water
and have none for the meal.
Strange, these thoughts that well up
in me. Could it be he has come?

Oh, such thoughts, such thoughts,
when I have bread to bake
and the hens to feed.

SAIPAN

As a boy, I ate mangoes and bananas
that grew around our Quonset hut,
and I split coconuts for milk
in a fort of broad-leaf palms.

Imagining a war I had missed
armed with a bayonet, a corroded holster,
and a piece of jawbone someone had found,
I waited to repel the Japanese.

I walked on burning feet
fifty yards to the beach, avoiding snarls
of seaweed, the gluey milk of sea slugs
and gazed to the edge of the world

past a neighbor's sailboat bobbing
its anchor pulling against the Pacific.
Beyond was an island, Managaha,
where failed bombs still ticked in the jungle.

A torpedoed Japanese freighter sat
arched on the coral reef along the horizon.
Wrapped in an algae skirt, its rusted sides
glowed like embers in the declining sun.

Now I pick the fruit of grown-up trees
where boyhood forts have fallen
from the weight of adult scenes:
shrapnel clouds block the Saipan sun;

families, arm in arm, leap from the cliffs;
panicked GIs in the blood-wrecked sand
outshriek the shrieks of a Banzai charge;
corpses ripen in the caves.

AN IRAQI SOLDIER

There he lies, lifeless, at dusk,
his trivial helmet blown away,
his body humped over a berme,

his sand-plastered face sideways
on an outstretched, pointing arm,
his eyes horrified. Shells explode.

This is not his war. No match
for the coalition, he holds his side,
his olive drab blackened with blood.

His stiffening arm points eastward
beyond smoke curling from the hatch
of a tank, past the glow of Baghdad,

across the desert of his ancestors,
over the ancient mountains of Asia,
across the Pacific, beyond a boy

in red shorts making sand castles
on the beach in San Francisco,
beyond the girl in Topeka, Kansas

playing hopscotch, past a teen
at the salad bar in Dayton, Ohio
reaching for tongs, her Sunday skirt

pulled against her thighs,
toward steps of the Pentagon
where a reporter scratches his neck

before the briefing on a breezy day
in the Tidal Basin where branches
of cherry trees explode into bloom.

STAUNTON-PARKERSBURG TURNPIKE

(Winter 1862)

I'm propped against a naked maple tree,
a wounded man abandoned in a field.
Some time ago, beneath a snowy sea,
My gun and shifting tracks were sealed.

A mute platoon of pines salutes the sky.
The silent subjects here are bound
to stay with me. Birches bow and sigh,
deferring to the wind and icy ground.

A solitary spruce accepts a screen
of powdered camouflage that lights
along its limbs and coaxes them to lean
in quiet homage to insistent rites.

Gray, denuded hardwood stands invite
an oak with rusty leaves still clinging on
to help them filter out the light.
A chill rolls in with dark, and day is gone.

I'm cuddled in a comforter of snow.
An aching heat in my upper half
has not let go. Propped on my bed I know
its twisted branches are my epitaph.

VOCABULARY

for Ryan

My son says, "kouwalli,"
and we know this to mean, "screwdriver."
He wants his daddy's kouwalli.
Though only two, he has a preference
for hand tools.

His kouwalli is far from scarred knuckles,
or the cusswords that shoot like cannonballs
at the slip from a rusted screw.

It is only a few weeks
and kouwalli is lost forever
from his word list. The jumble
has suddenly righted itself.

We are proud that our son
discovers words we use
to say what he means,
though they propel him
into the ordinary.

We smile and encourage him
as he surveys his kingdom
and names the animals.

BLUEBERRY PIE

The woodstove seemed to devour hardwood
this winter. We could not keep warm
when it was three degrees outside for a week.

My wife was concerned
because Abigail's lips were blue.
No matter how many logs I jammed
into the stove, the poor girl's lips were blue.

She seemed just fine
with her merry brown eyes
and red cheeks. She skipped
about the house and did not complain
of the cold. But we bundled her up
just the same.

It was a mystery, her blue lips
until late one afternoon
when the refrigerator door slammed.
"Alright," my wife said,
"who ate the blueberry pie?"

DYLAN TAKES THE FLOOR

At ten months, he is too heavy,
some think, to walk this soon.
He is a doughboy in diapers.
But with one chubby hand
he grips the couch end and rises.
His cheeks are pomegranates.

He stands on thighs thick as those
on T-Rex and growls. He shows a row
of four dangerous teeth. Then,
with blue eyes indifferent,
he flings aside a stuffed bear.

With arms ahead, he crosses the room,
surefooted as Frankenstein's monster,
then plops down. But soon he is up
fisting a bottle of milk.
With head back and bottle to his lips,
he is Louis Armstrong
reaching the high notes.

A BLIND MAN IN AUTUMN

The stick came waving before him
like a wand dazzling the sidewalk
with reflected sun. He followed,
in the maze of his dark world,
scaring grackles that hurried
in groups after seed. He blundered
onto aspen leaves arranged brilliantly
at his feet and passed by me
oblivious to my bright colors.
At the curb he poked at air and listened
poised like a cat sniffing a new room.
When he advanced, his stick moved
like a pendulum in its limited swing.
At the opposite curb, he ignored the irises
and missed the sculptured hedges.
When he tapped along the measured slabs,
he did not see the raked leaves
nor the row of fiery maples,
but he stopped suddenly
and leaned toward a dying elm.
In a while, he pulled close his collar
in the brisk air and moved on.
In the elm, a woodpecker
was tapping out a hollow tune.

BLUEBIRDS

Mount the birdhouse six feet off the ground
clear of the woods and facing an open field.

That was years ago. Only now, in this bluster
of April did bluebirds unpack their suitcases

and try out the cedar home. We are willing
to wait eternally for answers to the longings—

the images hoped for, the soul's endless throbs
and percolations. When light descends, the heart

opens like a tulip. You walk out one morning
where the grays and browns of winter bow

to dogwoods in bloom, forsythia, the redbud
and its unearthly purples, leaves everywhere,

green and from nowhere you can point to,
but there they are—robins on the lawn,

a red-headed woodpecker drumming
hallelujahs on the elm, and at the birdhouse,

bluebirds flashing their luminous wings
with colors flown in from some other world.

SNAPPING TURTLE

It was on the two-lane country road ahead
beside the woods, this armored dinosaur.
It had been turned out of the flooded creek
and was sure to find its way under car wheels.

I let the children out to see the snapper.
Big as an ash can lid, it turned to face us
with sharp beak, raised scutes on a black shell,
grey, spiked coat of mail on its thick neck,
and five-clawed paws padded like a goalie's.

With a stick about a finger thick, I tried to move it
by nudging the shell. The turtle wheeled, snapped
off a beakful of stick, then stared us down.
I tried again, but it spit the piece at us and hissed.

By then, cars were lining up. Two men,
one holding a bottle of beer, walked over.

"Them's good eatin'," he said. The other agreed.

The first handed his beer to the other,
then sauntered over to the snapper,
crouched behind it, then, with both hands,
grabbed its sides, but the turtle capsized.

In a second, the snapper fully extended its neck
and spun its black snout on the asphalt to right itself.
The skill of millions of years stared us in the face.

The snapper, too big for its hand-me-down shell,
turned, in its own good time, rowed across the asphalt
to the grassy edge near the creek, the scutes
of its shell gleaming like the shield of Achilles.
"Call me slow," he seemed to mean,
"but, by God, I will get there."

MEDITATIONS ON A BOWL OF RICE

for Sonja James

Boil two cups of water. Add cup of rice. Simmer until water is
absorbed.
Repeat as necessary. Feed half the world.

Who, in the delta of Tigris or Euphrates, Ganges, or Yangtze,
was the first to see a future in the seeds of tall, green marsh grass?

In some Asian languages, food means rice, rice food.
Among the Chinese, a form of greeting is "Eat rice?"

In southern China, fields of rice wave in the morning breeze.
Above, before an orange sky, the trumpeting of cranes.

Starchy carbohydrate. Supplement with soy, olive, or sesame oil.
Add protein—meat, fish, vegetables—in moderation. Sip rice wine.

Annual, worldwide rice production: one half billion metric tons—
much of this mountain of seed husks removed by the bare feet of
women.

In Sri Lanka, beside a mango grove, water buffaloes pull plow and
harrow.
The bronze plowman in white loin cloth feels dung between his toes.

Round, jointed stems with long, pointed leaves and edible seeds on
heads
of separate stalks grow tall in the fields beneath the terraced hills
of Bali.

Workers near Guangzhou, transplanting seedlings to flooded fields, push roots
into mud. For four millennia, in lush fields, workers bend their backs and sigh.

Drain fields. Take reaping knife, reed mat, and basket. Cut stalks.
Thresh rice to loosen hulls or winnow free of chaff by tossing in air above mat.

Savvy America plies the long grain in techno-paddies in Louisiana, Mississippi, Arkansas, Texas, and the Golden State. Whooping cranes dance in the fields.

At sunset, near Bangalore, an old farmer kneels: Lord, after a day-long fast,
I taste you in a bowl of steaming rice. When will you show me your face?

MEN ON MOWERS—EARLY FALL

Though many praise your sonnet, Mr. Frost,
I'd rather write a poem than mow the grass.
On Saturdays, my neighbors mount their steeds
and ride as reverent as Peter at Pentecost
across their acreage and burn up gas.
I have trees, a smaller lot, a wife who mows.
We push a Briggs & Stratton in the yard
with no attachment for dispensing seeds.
The fact is the sweetest dream that labor knows,
but every week it's back—long and green.
Did you learn that little adage at Harvard?
The handsome grass, cut into sinuous rows,
receives the whispering leaves. Halloween
is nearly here again. Let me roll up the hose.

MULCHING THE ROCK GARDEN

We'd already cleared vines and leaves
between the dogwood and slippery elms
on the upward slope behind the house.
We had irises in and mountain bluets.

We left the honeysuckle and arranged,
inside the tree line, thick slabs of brown shale.
To discourage grass, we laid out newspapers
before dumping the wheelbarrows of mulch.

There, kneeling in the bare earth, I stopped,
read headlines, parts of feature stories:
the high school junior, at the plate, recognized
for taking her team to the state softball finals;

the politician imploring us to remember her
and our children at the school board vote;
the Labrador retriever, tongue hanging,
pictured with a family for saving their toddler.

With a pitchfork and the respect I could muster,
I threw mulch on their faces, buried them,
the journalists' careful words, the model
beckoning in lingerie, the local, the national news.

BALLET LESSON

Lily writhes, her face contorted
from catching her finger in the car door.
She is six—too young to know such hurt.

She grips her hand. In her twisted face,
I see the pain of Dido, of Trojan women
holding their fallen men, their dying sons.

I kiss her hand. No cut, no blood.
She wipes her eyes, forgets her grief.
As we drive to class, she points out daffodils,

dogwood, redbud, forsythia that bloom
along this mountain road. Her pink-clad body
and blonde hair bounce on the car seat.

We follow the winding road to town
not looking too far ahead, nor behind,
but welcoming this warm, clear day. I pray

she will transform the pain of practice,
learn the plié, glissade, arabesque,
to greet her life en pointe, to pirouette,

to read and embrace in people's faces
the centuries of grief, the yearnings,
and yes, my little flower, to bloom.

TULIPS AT EASTER

after 9/11

I brought them to my wife
after a business trip to Manhattan
where it rained and rained
on a people rebuilding.

From dark soil in an earthen pot
rose seven stems, broad-leafed,
long and sturdy as corn stalks.

Above them, yellow-green tubes,
pencil thin and upright,
supported flowers closed
and bowed as monks at vespers.

On our oak dining table
in overcast skies, tulips
quietly passed Good Friday.

On Sunday, they awoke
their flowers cupped hands
offering hallelujahs,
their petals red as shed blood.

GRASS

(September 11, 2001)

As for man, his days are as grass:
as a flower of the field, so he flourisheth.
For the wind passeth over it, and it is gone;
and the place thereof shall know it no more.

PSALM 103:15, 16 KJV

Yes, Walt Whitman, *grass is the beautiful uncut hair of graves,*
and *the smallest sprout shows there is really no death.*
For out of the burnt ground comes life, from the ruptured seed
comes life,
and death does not wait at the end to arrest it, and death *ceas'd the
moment life appear'd.*

For I consider the thousands of species of grass, vascular plants,
the annual and perennial herbs, fibrous roots and rhizomes tunnel-
ing underground,
adapting in the habitable ranges of earth, some with little rain,
spreading gloriously over the prairies and plains of North America,
flourishing in the savannas and pampas of South America,
reaching to heaven in the steppes and plains of Eurasia, and in the
veldt of Africa.

For I consider the stems, hollow and swollen at the nodes,
the two-part leaves, the sheath surrounding the stem and a blade,
flat and linear,
the flowers unique in form, the blossoming subdivided into spikelets

with tiny florets like the daisy and dandelion and the dry, seedlike
grain, a caryopsis,

a corn of wheat that falls into the ground and dies and brings forth
much fruit.

For I consider the grass family providing the grain, the staple food
for mankind,

the feed for animals, domestic and wild, the cattle that graze upon
a thousand hills;

the meristems set back from the apex of the blade, yielding new cell
growth after the grazing,

the tenacious underground root systems—the beach grasses—that
prevent erosion

and the smell of mowed grass, incense in the summer air.

For I consider the cereal grasses—wheat, rice, corn, oats, barley, and
rye,

the hay and pasture plants—sorghum, timothy, bent grass, blue-
grass, orchard grass,

and the fescue, which adorn the lawns of America sprinkled with
clover and alfalfa,

the molasses and sugar from sugar cane and sorghum, the grain
liquors that warm the soul,

the bamboo and reeds that make and thatch the shelters of mankind,

the manna, like white coriander seed, that fed the Israelites in the
wilderness.

For I consider the intricacies of each blade, the microbiology of
seed plants,

the angiosperms, having leaves, stems, roots, and conducting tissue—

xylem and phloem—and seed-making ovules within the ovary, en-
closed in the pistil,

giving birth to the flowering plants, the cereal grains and other
grasses,

garden flowers and plants, common shrubs and trees, and roadside weeds,

all performing in secret their miracles, their cell divisions, their reaching for light.

Yes, Walt Whitman, *the dead are alive and well somewhere* and are as numerous as stars,

as numerous and diverse as the seed of Abraham. *All goes onward and outward;*

nothing collapses, and to die is different from what any one supposed, and luckier.

AT THE HOME DEPOT MADE FAMOUS
BY THE NORTHERN VIRGINIA SNIPERS

I'd stopped in during lunch hour
to look at appliances. I remembered
seeing the covered loading area in the news.
The cranial blood of the cancer survivor
has long since seeped into the pavement.

Thousands have trod on the place
where she lay beside the trunk of her vehicle,
her careful purchases insignificant
in their shopping bags. She did not survive
the trunk shot from a Chevy.

Here they are today, the busy shoppers,
loading their mulch, their 2x4s,
their bathroom fixtures, scores
of citizens gritting their teeth,
putting their shoulders to the task
of home improvement. The tragedy is past.

For weeks before the snipers were nabbed,
I'd hesitate before stepping from my car
at the office. My wife said to bob my head,
make it hard to keep in crosshairs.

Now, down the aisles, fellow shoppers
avoid my stare. Their furtive eyes scan price tags,
shelves of nails. I zigzag my shopping cart

like a Navy destroyer in the Pacific,
maneuver away from the sub's torpedoes.

The shoppers can't bear to wait in lines.
They expect the salespeople to know everything.
Behind me, a display of power drills, bumped
by a child, crashes down. People's feet click
on the tile floor around me. They listen for the slap
of a rifle bolt, are ready to take cover.

LUCY AND LILY

For a year, I'd wake and pray I was dreaming,
but it was always our blue-eyed twins crying.
They'd refuse to sleep or let us sleep.
They'd be starving or wriggling in wet diapers.
I'd roll over, pretend I had more time,
but hear my wife always up warming bottles.

The stars are easier to count than bottles
we've filled or washed. We were dreaming,
as newlyweds, to think we'd give our free time
to having children. I've never liked the crying
or the thousand challenges posed by diapers.
I see them still—leaping like sheep in my sleep.

The twins are three now, and they sleep
in beds in their own room. Gone are bottles,
the rocking, the jumbo packs of diapers.
Their nights are long and filled with dreaming,
yet at bedtime, there is defiant crying
of twins who must hug their mother one more time.

As parents of six, we have done our time.
We know the torments of interrupted sleep
and how a twin can trigger tandem crying
or how one is tempted to whiskey a baby bottle.
We've put aside some dreams, yet admit to daydreaming,
remembering babies in tiny caps and hospital diapers.

Lucy and Lily, crouching, are fitting diapers
on baby dolls. For all of them, it is bedtime.
Soon, twins and babies are in bed dreaming.
Blonde hair frames angelic faces as twins sleep.
Beside them, plastic babies grip plastic bottles.
Exhausted, we hope to hear no crying.

Lucy runs up to say her sister is crying.
Adventures follow ones we've outgrown, like diapers.
Now we read labels on medicine bottles.
Lily has banged her head for the hundredth time.
Children's Tylenol should help us all sleep.
In bed, I listen but drift back to days of dreaming.

Do echoes of crying subside, given the time,
as midnight diapers give way to stretches of sleep?
Does the end of bottles revive in the heart the dreaming?

LABOR DAY WEEKEND 2005

Early morning on the wood deck
behind our windowed sun room
on a cushioned wrought iron chair

and surrounded by hickories and oaks
on our hidden acre, I am reading poetry.
The children are asleep. My wife

prepares meals in our huge kitchen.
A breeze tempers the sun that warms
my drowsy face and sleeveless arms.

A butterfly, a Red-spotted Purple,
lands on my finger and probes the skin
with its long, flexible proboscis.

A hummingbird, above the deck rail,
beside the potted impatiens, noses,
in turn, into each red blossom.

Soon, the butterfly lifts off, not finding,
on my skin, its mainstays—rotted fruit,
animal dung—and glides past the windows.

Inside, a CNN TV reporter mouths a story
to accompany apocalyptic images
of a war-ravaged equatorial country.

Labor Day Weekend 2005

Cameras pan the blank faces of survivors
who wade through house-strewn streets.
Flushed from homes, they cling to rooftops.

Behind them is the Superdome. This
is New Orleans. This is America,
land of plenty. Look what it took

for us to see you—brothers, sisters—
scratching out your lives under the dome
of a dark and receding heaven.

HEADLESS BARBIES

for Lucy and Lily

"Daddy, can you put the head on this damn thing?"
my daughter says. She stands next to my desk
holding a smiling head of thick, platinum hair
in one hand, a chiffon-gowned body in the other.

"Honey, please don't talk like that," I say, knowing
her frustration. I twist the hollow head of hair
onto the plastic stump of neck. My daughter thanks me
and runs off to join her twin sister in their room.

The twins turned five today. Curls of sun-bleached
blonde hair crown blue-eyed, smiling faces.
Tanned from the summer, they play dress-up
and wear princess gowns and my wife's high heels.

They pull the heads off, not to harm the dolls,
but to change outfits. It's easier to switch heads
than to work the buttons and elusive snaps
on dresses, blouses, or Barbara Eden pantaloons.

Pulling off a head beats guiding tiny sleeves
over plastic arms or pulling pedal pushers
over pointed toes always ready to receive high heels.
My wife and I stand by to twist on heads.

Headless Barbies

One minute you're a blonde with blue eyes,
in a crimson gown, then pop, and you have freckles,
red hair, and green eyes. And the dolls, through it all,
never lose their smiles, their unblinking happiness.

The dozen or so dolls, for the most part naked,
headless torsos with perfect breasts and legs,
are aesthetically challenged by swivel hips
and legs that show the lines of ball and socket joints.

Nevertheless, they lie in an oval, green suitcase,
outstretched arms and hands ever beckoning,
as the twins, at ease among torsos, mix and match
from an array of gowns and bodiless heads of hair.

Though dolls in a doll's world, the twins erupt
into savagery, at times, and wrestle for gowns or heads.
Sweet as they are, they bite each other and pull hair.
Their Solomon, I stand by ready to arbitrate—

as I will in years to come when their adolescent bodies
are unacceptable to themselves, their hair, their clothes
are never quite right. I look into the dark without blinking,
and practice smiles plastic and vacuous as space.

SAGO

"Please, Doctor, I feel a pain.
Not here. No, not here. Even I don't know."

CZESLAW MILOSZ, FROM "I SLEEP A LOT"

They never asked to be born here,
but, in this rolling country, coal runs
deep in their veins. Like their fathers
and their fathers' fathers, they grip
their wife-packed lunches and go
to the mines, or they turn their backs
on king coal and seek the exotic,
the far away. Each has cut his groove,
has found the poison he must drink
to survive. Down into the deep womb
of their beginnings they go, dust to dust,
their black faces glistening in lamplight
as shadows against the dark face of coal—
their wives, anguished, asking why,
when a man, at night, spits up blood,
he goes back down that dank hole.
And we, unknowing, on the outside, rich
in mountain air, see into that gaseous,
cold space, into the dark face of our future.
We will wait for you. Come, tell us
what you found on the other side, whether
one day our faces, like yours, will shine.

FISHING

for Meredith

My six-year-old daughter,
shorter than the rod she holds,
is anxious for instruction.
It is our first day beside the lake
after winter.

I bloodworm her hook,
say to hold the reel's button down
with her thumb, and to release it
when she's swung the rod toward water.
She gets it right off.

"When you see the bobber disappear,"
I say, "give a little pull on the rod."

The bass she caught cared little
that it was her first fish.
A green, blank eye lolled
as I pulled the hook,
and as I threw back the bass,
the don't-do-me-any-favors tail swished.

Next day I cannot rise from bed.
I'm thinking it's a stroke, a little death.
My left side is paralyzed,
yet with no drooping jaw, no spittle.
It is sore muscles from casting.

FISHING

I am thankful death creeps
into our lives, giving us time to adjust.

As we cast forth our lines,
our sun-lit lives float and bob
on delicate rings and undulations,
unaware of what prize they might land
or of what line-snapping jaws
might be opening.

So I take hold forever of this scene:
my daughter's rod bent toward water,
the bobber dipping down,
and her determined cast, as she reels in,
as she feels on the line the telegraphic hum,
as she wrestles with the unseen.

PEREGRINE

Words move, music moves
Only in time; but that which is only living
Can only die. Words, after speech, reach
Into the silence.

T.S. ELIOT – "BURNT NORTON"

A camera pans the western hills on fire
as glowing forests crackle to the end.
In time, the ashen earth, the animal bones
will part, defer to a million sprouts beginning
their lush, exotic lives, where even the rose
can dance in new air. I watch with humility

at what might have been, for humility,
the poet says, is endless. Yet in the fire
went the oaks, the firs and pines, the rose
as people go and nations move to their end
and fertilize the ground for an age beginning,
new seed at root in the cavities of bones.

The memories of coupling may live in bones
where flesh and blood are gone. In humility,
they bide their time for the close of beginning—
what our bones tell us is so, what the fire
in the breast hopes for—an end of end—
a still point where no one must water the rose.

We have spilled millions of words on the rose.
Its petaled beauty, as love, endures in our bones,
as we maintain a scaffold of meaning to the end
unwilling to live without purpose. In humility,
we try to abide in darkness, but build a fire
to find our way in a cave to the beginning.

A falcon clears the nest of its own beginning,
but, in time, must land. So, too, the lovely rose
can prick. We find solace in the pain of fire
where pain purges, brings healing to the bones
and, in the sages, compassion, humility—
a suffering that trusts in a meaningful end.

Yet we practice war and death without end,
a centennial sadness from the beginning
where people hate and plot, disdain humility,
take to the streets, trample the garden rose
and, with sticks, beat each other's bones.
Let us throw the sticks into the fire.

In the end, I see the rose as more than a rose
despite the thorns. As for the beginning, my bones
teach me humility and speak with tongues of fire.

NURSERY DUTY

The children, clinging,
listened to the coos of soothing parents
who patiently persuaded them
to loosen little finger grips
and not confuse this with abandonment.
The words subdued them all
except for one or two
who refused to let us woo them
to contentment in the toy-filled room.
The parents tiptoed toward their pews
for worship and the Eucharist
and left the under-fives to work it through
among themselves
and us,
the sitters.
The caution drifted off,
relaxed the mood, and soon
the bolder ones began to move
among the blocks, the books,
the wooden stools.
A single crier stood indignant and apart
to brood.
A sympathizer chose to feed on a thumb
for the hour, and snoozed.
An infant girl,
not long from mother's womb,
rolled,
clutched a plastic donut,
grinned and drooled.

A brown-haired boy
approached me in that room,
spoke a paragraph or two
in some tongue unknown to me,
then withdrew.

A man of two skittered by,
his pampered bottom huge,
and wrestled from a colleague
a rubber tool.

Mostly they were amused,
these matrimonial fruits,
and were good.

LOVE POEM

I lean over in bed,
prop one arm up with the other,
scratch your back, turn my head
to see the ten o'clock news.

Two of our six are brushing teeth,
laying out school clothes. Who knows
where the others are? You'd think
having one would trigger birth control.

They peer in or barge into our room
hoping to catch us at something.
With them around, how could we?
How did we get six of them?

I switch hands and resume, hanging on
with a finger or two. Oh for the days
when we were young and fresh
when, as newlyweds, in our love rush,

in the basement apartment we rented
from a violinist, we snapped
the box spring frame. What operas
we mounted, what crescendos.

For twenty years, you, rock hard,
have endured the foul weather
I've rained on you. Forgive me.
I have taken you for granite.

VIOLA

In the den where I work each morning
where outside the blue curtain the mountain
rises its green clothing hiding deer
its morning fog bringing with it the notes
of a viola a viola being played somewhere
beyond the lake where someone plays a viola
with a morning song the low notes flowing
from the mountain across the lake
and in the fog moving slowly muffled by rain
the viola moving toward me as I write
my morning assignments as I rub my eyes
in the morning a viola moves across the lawn
comes past the holly brings low notes
into the den where I work each morning
a viola bringing its loneliness
from the mountain across the lake
past the deer grazing on green lawns
a viola comes into the den where I rub my brow
each morning in the den where I work
a viola brings its low and lonely voice
to me each morning.

RYAN'S CHAIR

The oak ladderback, joints caked
with yard-sale glue, is older by far
than my nine-year old, but it fits his desk.
He rocks between G.I. Joe and his homework,
on the four legs, angles on two legs
toward the sharpener, grinds his pencil to a nub,
eyes the point. The legs stutter on the floor
above us as he heats up the eraser.

The boy cannot sit still, and I cannot bear
the image of cracked and splintering wood.
I may try a rocker next, of cast iron.

I reiterate my parameters. "Sit still!" I say.
"Pay attention to your work."
But he is miles ahead of me, exploring worlds.
He cannot sit still.

I fix the limp-joint chair when it rocks by itself.
Panhead screws, numerous as studs on a biker's jacket,
protrude from the rounded legs. Steel "L" brackets
reinforce the back. The seat is bound beneath
with truss plates. Carpenter glue, thick as syrup,
fills the joints.

I hear him in his room, unstoppable,
cantering through multiplication,
leaning into and away from cursive,
galloping through amphibians, riding hard
through fields, the wind in his hair.

CLEANING THE RANGE TOP

The wet cloth grazes electric coils
not yet cool from supper. They spit.
With a thumbnail, I scrape enamel
to loosen baked-on patties of tomato sauce—
like my mother—who cooked and scoured
and scrubbed for seven children.

I'd lean against the wall and spill
my teenage woes. She'd load the dishwasher,
wipe countertops, scrape dried food
with a thumbnail.

"Have the guts to step out on your own,"
she'd say. All this from a lady who, at eighteen,
had given up England for an American flyboy.
The polish on her nails was chipped.

Our youngest coughs from her bed, but sleeps.
My wife's slippers click on the oak floor
across from our room; she pushes open
the bedroom door to listen for breathing.

Down the hall with our youngest son
she discusses ways to shake a bully.
My tactics are normally wrong,
will get him sent to the principal.

Cleaning the Range Top

I wipe countertops, think of my wife,
of sacrifices, of my mother working
her fingers to the bone.

THE POPINDOO HAT MAN

Part I. Prayer for My Father

The name's origin is forgotten,
and it means nothing apart from us,
but the kids all remember whooping it
as we swooped down the stairs like Indians
when you returned from work:
"The Popindoo Hat Man is home
the Popindoo Hat Man."
I hovered close to you waiting for "Chief,"
the title conferred on me
and the graze of your face
against my war-painted cheek.

"Your father has more talent in his little finger
than Da Vinci had in both hands,"
my English mother said.
I'd let my friends in to see
canvases arranged and the easel.
When I posed for your art class,
students painted in the baseball mitt
and the grin under the visor of my ball cap.
I was picturing my father
winning jitterbug contests, twirling
my dark-haired mother with his little finger.

Your portrait of me gazes with eyes
trying to imagine you, gentle man,
daring to crouch with flak jacket

loose on your skinny boy's shoulders
in daylight raids over Berlin
aiming your artist's eyes at Messerschmitts
screaming with machine gun rounds
as you swung your mounted fifty calibers
spitting from the wounded side of a B-17.
When your marriage died, we thrashed and cried,
but some of us survived the crash dive.

I study the works in your studio
where a portrait looks from the easel,
a voluptuous barmaid smiling
with an unfinished mouth.
She promised payment
as she swirled your drinks,
and my head swirls
to think of the spin, the dive,
the altitude lost. In a mirror,
I see a self-portrait behind me,
perhaps in front of me.

The nurses shake their white-hatted heads
not believing you are still alive:
your numbers went to the top of the chart.
"You can't live without a liver," one said
as she turned and squeaked away on clinical shoes.
The bilirubin and ammonia that cloud your blood
are coming down. Though you lie in a fog
drifting in toward me and back out again to sleep,
you grasp for the humor you have lived by
and greet me with an uplifted palm:
"I Chief Yellow Eyes."

Your wife sits by the bed.

She is not my mother,
but I hug her and stand there
with my grievances plain as scalps
drying on my belt,
but you joke about the Man Upstairs,
who is pulling you through,
and I clear my throat and pray,
father of eleven children,
that you will rise like an eagle,
perhaps circling at first, and fly.

Part II. Personal Representative

My artist father, still a young man
at seventy-three, died in November: lover
of his eleven children, lover of women,
lover of the play of words,
lover of Irish whiskey,
lover of the seashore.
I, first son, and court-appointed
Personal Representative, sift
through his mail, bank books, wallet,
private files, change on his dresser,
to close out his life officially.

A court has granted me authority
to pay my father's bills. The banks
have released his funds, convinced
I am the genuine article.

The Popindoo Hat Man

A credit card letter exudes disappointment
in you, Valued Customer, whose credit
in the past has been without reproach.
But circumstances being what they are,
Valued Customer,
we must cancel your credit card
for non-payment on your account.

A letter to my English mother
declares her beneficiary of life insurance.
She has been dead for twenty years.
My father, slow at paperwork, never left her,
divorce or no divorce. He, over beers,
would sing of her brown eyes, the gutsy lady,
her raising seven children, and how, years
after he'd gone, his heart ached
to turn her athletic, cancerous body
in a hospital bed, those lovely legs,
that English laugh, till death us do part.

Pension, stocks, bank accounts,
life insurance, easel, canvases,
brushes, pastels, prize paintings,
binoculars, cameras, photographs,
end tables, lamps, bed, chairs,
the leather couch, the Buick,
blankets, sheets, towels,
dishes, pots, pans, socks,
shoes, keys, rings, watch.
How does one divide another
eleven ways?

THE POPINDOO HAT MAN

From his things I have kept
a briefcase, a camelhair coat,
a tweed cap, a belt,
a three-battery flashlight.
His hat on my head, his belt
looped in my pants, his coat on me,
his briefcase in my right hand,
I step into the dark to meet bankers,
creditors, insurance reps.
In my left hand, I hold the flashlight,
seeking my way.

B-17 OVER BERLIN

You were left waist gunner on this bomb run
we discover sixty years later. A niece researched
the 306th Bomb Group, Eighth Air Force,
and found your name on the roster.

On 22 March 1944, your plane had taken flak
at twenty-five thousand feet over the best defenses
in Europe. Your flying fortress dropped behind the
formation. Number four engine had lost controls.
Number three had a runaway propeller. Number two
was losing oil. Number one carried the load.

With a dead right wing, the captain trimmed the plane
and flew with the right wing cocked up thirty degrees.
You lost altitude, but stayed with your fifty calibers
waiting for Messerschmitts. You jettisoned gear.

By Zuider Zee, you were at four thousand feet.
At one hundred feet above the Dutch coast, citizens
waved encouragement from the ground.

Across the channel, the runway at the British base
was short. The B-17 barreled off the concrete
and into a couple of sheds, but stopped.
Weeks later, after you'd married an English girl,
you went aloft to complete your twenty-five missions.
Your subsequent wounds were all internal.

You—father, artist, gentle man, great wit—live on

in your eleven children. Sorting, though we are,
through the wreckage of your marriages, the rubble,
the bric-a-brac of our childhoods, we thank you
for heroism in war, are sorry our parents inhaled
the stench of Europe where men and women—

winners and losers—crawled from the ruins
of their bombed-out futures, buried what they'd seen,
and—brick by brick—rebuilt the story of their lives,
their nations and went forth dreaming and hopeful
into the smoky, doubtful air.

HYMN TO MY WIFE DOING LAUNDRY

Though hampers overflow in morning light,
you tackle several pungent loads a day
and measure out your life by dark and white.

Our youngest drop their dirty clothes at night
on bathroom floors, then bathe and dress to play,
though hampers overflow in morning light.

We ask our busy teens to help. "Yeah, right.
I'm tired of being your freakin' maid," they say.
You measure out your life by dark and white

and sort and fold your memories, a rite
you pass with clothes, then put them all away,
though hampers overflow in morning light.

The piles of folded clothes, all fresh and bright,
appear somehow in chests of drawers that way
and measure out your life by dark and white.

With iron will, you spritz and press, then fight
with tangled hangers as your hair turns gray.
Though hampers overflow in morning light,
you measure out your life by dark and white.

SQUARE KNOTS

for Ryan

My son and I practice tying knots. He seeks
a merit badge. I was a Scout, and on my honor
I've made many promises to God, to country, to
people tied to me. I've been tying knots all my life.

Only now can I say precisely the steps to make a
square knot—or reef knot—every time and not
the unstable granny. A square knot requires rope ends
parallel to the rope's standing part to avoid slippage.

Sailors use square knots to reef sails to cross spars.
My life has been trial and error, but I chant the formula
as my son crosses over two whipped ends of rope:
"Right over left and under. Left over right and under."

Your belly knots up in these moments of clarity, and
you desire to go back to recover severed lines, the
opportunities, the devastation you've made of
relationships, the bitterness, the scenes in public.

You haul in and tie down what you can, live
with the lanyards flapping in air, ripped sails,
dull lashes from a storm-torn past. I wish for him
merit badges and a life not haunted by loose ends.

OLYMPICS

On TV, we see the white slopes
of Torino where cross-country skiers
in threes—one behind another—
lean in unison into a penguin walk,
their bent-out skis making birds' feet
in the snow. Their faces are strained
with resolve, their ski poles metronomes
as they push off side to side—uphill.
Every bit of their being is focused
on the peak where, once there, they glide
into a valley to where it's uphill again
and back to the penguin walk.
It is windy and cold. Their minds
are on silver and gold. I ask you
to recall our Ford Torino, our first car—
used. We were young and poor; now
we are old and poor. The Torino—huge,
ugly and sky blue—carried us through,
its vinyl roof pealed and leprous.
It was reliable and roomy, enough
for a row of baby car seats. Here,
in our family room, on Valentine's Day,
it is time to hold hands, relax our tight,
wind-blown faces and glide, glide
to the next hill. Together, for twenty-three
years, we have won much gold.

RICE

for Saradha

A friend from India
tells her daughter, Niranjana,
not to waste her rice
for in her next life—her janma—
she will return as an ant
to learn the value of food
by hoisting grains.

At supper, my English mother
speaks through me:
Don't waste your food;
millions are starving in India.

My American children,
ignorant of want, of karma,
tell me to ship their unfinished food
overseas. They have no fear
of ants, of souls returning,
of endless births, yet I press
on them biblical injunction,
knowing they will serve a variation
of this meal to their children.

Niranjana thinks of ants,
their colonies, the workers,
those hills of rice,
of her soul, all those souls

learning to shed desire,
and she answers:
"That will be fine.
I will return as an ant
if I can be the queen."

DRIVING RANGE

for Dylan

We are here because a neighbor gave my son,
nine and in fourth grade, an old set of clubs.
I tried golf many years ago, but had no patience for it.

The driver is too long for him, yet, devoid of deference,
he claims he will better me. In an age of reverence,
I worshiped my father. I am grey at the temples,
but ready for my son. My driver is longer than his.

He cannot know how, in his grade, in Catholic school,
I taught my brother the skills of an acolyte. Using
a cardboard square as pall to cover a drinking glass,
the chalice, I recited to him my responses in Latin.

A white-haired man next to us drives balls farther
than both of us. I say it has been twenty-five years
since I've hit a golf ball, that I never learned the game.

"Life is too short," he says. "You have to find time
to do the things you want." I nod and think of things
I wish I'd done. Golf is not one of them.

After two baskets of balls, we reach the 200-yard flag.
My son's face glistens with sweat. His hair is wet
at the temples. I say "Great," when he connects.
He is ready for what comes. He swings hard.

BIRD FEEDER, BIRD BATH

All summer, until the blue jays crash
the party with their jarring *jay jay—jay jay,*
finches, purple and gold, and sparrows
partake at the tree-hung mini-house,
its open sides dispensing seed, a mix
that brings them all: chickadees
and their *chickadee, see-dee, see-dee;*
titmice and juncos. A Carolina wren,
brown with white stripe behind its eye,
joins the party with *TEA kettle, TEA kettle.*

A white-breasted nuthatch hops down an oak
picking for bugs. A squadron of Eastern bluebirds
fans out to poplars around the pedestalled bath.
They sing *turee, turee,* their blue coats luminous
and Saks Fifth Avenue amid the greens and browns.
House wrens forage beneath the feeder
where a squirrel had scattered seed
by leaping to the roof from a hickory branch.
A pair of mourning doves enjoys a coo-ool bath.

For days, against our rear windows, a cardinal—
we think he's drunk on fermented pokeberries—
has flown again and again into the closed panes.
What-cheer, cheer, cheer, what-cheer he sings.
Salut! You black-faced, orange-billed redbird,
you red-mitered high Churchman, unhinged.
Yes, we see through a glass darkly. You,

fellow pilgrim, wine bibber, Salut! Carry on
as I do each day despite life's repeated whacks
to my beak. What we lack in temperance
we hold hands down in fortitude.

ODE TO MAN WITH BACKHOE

for Henry Taylor

He makes it look easy, his skill
in working the handful of levers,
in shifting his boots on the pedals.
The three-hundred-pound bucket hangs
limp-wristed as he swings the arm.
He's confident as a child
digging in sand.

I lean over the footings to watch
for wires, the underground power
to the house. Ballerina fingers
probe the ground.

Behind me the hydraulic arm flexes;
its greased steel gleams in the sun
as the diesel thumps and smokes
and is the only sound.
I point to where the man should dig.

I am sure the backhoe is in good hands,
but I look back when the bucket comes close.
The operator wears overalls and a ball cap.
He's gray at the temples.
"I won't hit you but once,"
he yells and grins.

Ode to Man with Backhoe

I imagine being filliped into eternity,
explaining to St. Peter how I got mesmerized
as the huge, knobbed tires embossed the ground,
by the way the man inched toward the block wall,
dug the bucket in and scooped out
a hundred years.

I think of the years the man
has been lifting dirt,
how he practiced in open spaces,
jerking the gears, seeing the bucket sprawl,
and how, each night, he parks the yellow steel,

its long arm stretched across the dig,
the lethal bucket still as stone,
and how each morning he starts the diesel,
guides the bucket to a chalk line,
and digs for his life.

SLUG

For Thou madest us for Thyself,
and our heart is restless,
until it repose in Thee.

St. Augustine, *Confessions*

A glint on the plywood sub floor
catches your eye in the August sun.
You've happened on a coin.
You imagine doubloons as you pick it up—

there must be more of them—
but it's a steel knockout plug,
a slug punched from an electrical box
by electricians who wired the house
and moved on.

You pick up the quarter-sized plug,
worthless like millions before this one
swept off sub floors with sawdust,
bent nails, wood scraps, and soda cans
to be bulldozed underground.

You are not in this for the money,
yet you look when a glint catches your eye.
You scrape your hand across plywood,
its grain and patterns rough,
and scoop up sawdust, its pine smell fresh.
You are rooted in this Virginia clay.

SLUG

At quitting time, you unclip your tool belt,
roll up extension cords, cradle your thermos,
pack your truck, head home glad
you have finished one more click of mileage
on your sojourn here.

Yet you know the next time you glimpse a light
in a roughed-in house under roof,
its studded walls skeletal,
its plywood floors shimmering with sun,
you will turn your head to see
the shining city, the streets of gold.

A BRICKLAYER'S HELPER

Construction workers, I was told,
are built like brick walls.
Impatient to put some beef on
my boyhood bones, I found myself,
one summer, on the carrying end
of a mortar hod. It seemed
the bricklayers were always calling
for mud in their mortar pans,
or block, or tongs full of bricks.
Setting up scaffolds was like
trying to step lightly in quicksand.
I licked the sweat from my lips
and cursed the sun, the flies,
and stumbled under the weight
of 2 X 12 scaffold boards
that ripped into my shoulders.
Beads of blood, like epaulets,
spotted my tee shirt
as I pulled my plunger-feet
along behind me. I cried out,
in my toil, in my sweat,
"Christ, this is hard work."

TROWELING

Cement the door to keep my brother out.
This drying mortar makes it hard to hear
his call. It's not his needy hand I fear.
It's the gnawing, unremitting doubt
of every getting safely nestled in.
The planes are here and trembling in my ears.
I pray, oh God, you stop my brother's tears.
Protect me, bricks, from this approaching din.
The bombs have ceased their pounding on the mark.
I'm still alive. My walls withstood the shock.
I hear the solemn ticking of my clock
and fear the hollow quiet of the dark.
The creeping cold has settled by degrees
to laugh at me upon my aching knees.

SEARCH ENGINE

I.

On a whim, I searched the Internet
for my name. The first appearance
was an Irishman, age twenty-five,
who, in 1859, in Dublin, California,
while working on the roof of a church
he was helping to build, fell to his death.
This young Catholic is distinguished
by having St. Raymond's graveyard
established for him. Fell from the roof.
Got buried where he lay. The Irish
are never far from poetry.
Among the turf-bound residents
are successful gold rushers, settlers,
many of Dublin's hardy founders,
members of the Donner Party.

You can just see the trail
to this stagecoach crossroads
from the blighted potato fields
of Ireland, these pioneers,
their eyes looking past
their famine-hardened bodies,
the squalor and fevers of steerage,
the women keening at the loss
of a child, the trek across America
to Dublin for a pot of gold
all the while blaming themselves

and their sins for their misfortunes.
So St. Raymond's had to be built,
despite the tragedy. Tom,
you would have liked to kneel
on those redwood floors alongside
the grateful, mystified survivors
offering their songs of praise.

II.

In ten years of carpentry,
I have set up and climbed scaffolding,
shingled houses, church roofs,
refurbished steeples, have slid once
from a tar-papered roof in a gust
and afternoon rain, landed feet first
on a deck below, have shingled
where the sun bubbled roof tar,
made tools too hot to touch,
have found my way in this land,
have knelt on church floors,
have prayed hard for wages,
for family, for friends.

This building cathedrals is an old story
really, the slippery roofs a nuisance,
but part of the job. I have a great ease
with ladders and scaffolding. As I climb
each day toward heaven, I breathe in
the clear air, and my hands grasp
the rungs. Yet the old foundations

continue to crumble beneath me,
so I pray hard for all of us.
It's only then I have a fear of falling.

BREAKING A TOOTH

Three carpenters lie in a crawlspace
below a wood floor beam rotted and sagged.
The owner allowed a toilet to leak for years
in the bathroom above. The toilet lists.

Do people choose to ignore their lives
unraveling around them? Did he think the leak
would heal itself, the floor suddenly go dry?
We place a twenty-ton jack under the beam.

I pump the steel rod to hoist the jack.
Under the beam, we stack brick and block.
The floor groans. We will shore it up, replace it,
re-set the toilet, reverse years of drip, drip, drip.

As the beam reaches a hair shy of level, a block
explodes from the weight. A chunk snaps off
half of my right front tooth. With my tongue,
I feel a freeway and belly crawl for the exit.

Outside, I brush dirt from my coveralls,
announce my displeasure to three counties.
Into my truck mirror, I smile, realize my IQ
has dropped forty points. My tooth for a toilet.

My students don't know I stop at Ray's Texaco
after a day of carpentry, brush off sawdust, change
into a suit, arrive on campus as the professor
to teach a night class. My kingdom for a tooth.

BREAKING A TOOTH

The dentist is skilled and replaces in minutes
what took thirty years to grow. He bonds
a composite of plastic and silicone to the tooth
and shapes it with a whirring wheel.

I leave his office and take my place with others
all over the world who have been trying for years
to tell us they never intended for their lives
to turn out this way.

BEER CANS

for Dave Gillam

The attic was hot even in May
as we struggled up century-old stairs
with wallboard and rolls of insulation.
We ripped out old ceiling plywood, flimsy
and not enough to beat the winter.
From the hollows of overhead joists,
dusty beer cans rolled onto our heads.

We imagined carpenters in the Thirties
getting hammered at noon on beers,
dedicating their work to remodeling crews
destined to shuffle in years down the road.
We were reverent. Those cans had been filled
and emptied before our birth.

We collected cone top American cans,
an empty six-pack of Pabst, a golden Bud,
some whiskey bottles. We laughed, knowing
those carpenters, how they'd lighted Luckies,
made cracks about Mary Lou, and cussed
in an attic, sweltering for wages.

On the Bud can, the red "A," the black eagle,
the rigid steel were perfect save for a pair
of church key holes. These signatures,
these stories, privy to members of the trades,
inspired us to lift a few beers of our own.

Beer Cans

Before tacking on the new drywall
to seal the echoes of our hammers and saws
behind the blankness of a gypsum wall,
we lined up a row of aluminum empties:
pop-top Miller cans mute but ready
to survive the rust of another Deluge.

BOTTLE COLLECTING

In sneakers thick with creek mud,
we waited for workers to knock off
and surveyed the construction site
from a dirt mound, a half-eaten apple
from the backhoe's bites.

A yellow earthmover on monstrous wheels
plunged across the clearing,
its steel belly packed with orange clay.
A diesel thumped and smoked
as a dozer tipped a pine stump.

As the April sun lowered, we searched
for bottles, but found arrowheads
partly exposed in the patterned ground
the cleated tires had left. Crystals
of splintered amethyst speckled the clay.

Suddenly we were archeologists
treading on ground where Red Men lay.
We were alive with the Cherokee,
chipping quartz, letting fly
our feathered arrows, too young

to read, in the passing shapes of clouds,
smoke signals that formed and dispersed,
as they had over those braves before us,
as they will long after we lie down,
blood brothers on beds of clay.

TO ST. PETER

(after Herbert)

The cock crowed
as you denied
all
and let them all
deride Him
while you fled
to hide.

You abode
still
in your lie
as they spiked Him
to a tree,
stripped,
and hoisted up for all
to see.

The cock crowed;
still,
you kept aside
and let them all
divide Him
flesh from life. Ay,

Peter,
ill from the load
of your lie,

To St. Peter

you wept
as He bled
dry
from crown and side.

And I,
bowed,
do hide,
for daily my
briny will
salts His side.

STONES

Sticks and stones, milestones
in the Stone Age.

Stonehenge, stone worshipers' stones;
stone crushers for the stone cutters.

The Pietà, David and Moses:
stone worshipers.

The egotist's touchstone: his birthstone;
the reverend's, brimstone.

The man safe behind his stone walls
bruised his foot on a peach stone.

There is Jackson standing like a stone wall.

Perseus stood stone still as Medusa's face,
in his shield, shone.

Sisyphus, stone roller, shy a stone's throw:
his millstone.

Crazy Horse, stone faced,
buried the soldiers under stone:
arrowheads, spearheads and tomahawks:
bloodstones.

Stones

The executioner honed his ax on a whetstone.
Thomas More, in the stone tower,
contemplated tombstones. His sovereign,
in the stone castle, sat among gemstones,
stone deaf.

Stephen, stone bruised,
lay stone dead at the feet of Saul,
stone cold. Saul,
leaving no stone unturned,
had cast no stones.

Pilate, his hands washed in a stone bowl,
waved off the Jew, his steppingstone.
The soldiers, like stone,
stood before the rolling tombstone
blinded by the light of the Cornerstone.

NO ONE IN PARTICULAR

A wrinkled face of black remorse
removes his hat and takes a seat
beside the bar, in stinking heat.
He'll have the same again, of course.
He sits alone, a taken pawn.
The swirls of smoke around his head
remind him that his love is dead.
He kissed the wound, but she was gone.
He'll drink until they close the bar.
He's done it now for many years.
The drinking helps to drown the tears
and hide the ugly, guilty scar.

THIRTY-NINE CICADA WINGS

Lily, seven, collected them from our grass
where they'd spun down from the trees.

Orange membranes of the outer wings sweep
into a cathedral arch. Fifteen inner panes,

like cellophane, are framed by the same orange leading.
The panes, a mix of long ovals and zig-zag ends,

fill the outer edge like adjacent counties. She knows
the grown-ups live for only a week or two and says

it doesn't make sense to have babies, then die.
It's too soon to discuss the brief candle of our lives.

They're an odd mix of parts, not what you'd expect
after seventeen years underground sucking on tree roots:

blunt, wide heads; protruding red beads for eyes;
a stout, orange-black body tied to high church wings.

And the male with its famous singing thorax.
With only a week to court, procreate and sign off,

the thorax drumming must be enough for the ladies,
the shrill song. The wingless, scaly nymphs fall

from tree to ground and dig in to synch their clocks
for the day of resurrection.

SPRING CONCERT AT THE MIDDLE SCHOOL

for Abigail

The jazz band swings the hall with Glenn Miller.
Pudgy boys stand in a row, trumpet a volley.
Girls with saxophones respond with pizzazz.
A snare drum chick-a-choon, chick-a-choons.

Mellow notes slide remarkably from trombones.
You tap your feet, snap your fingers, never mind
your cramped seat, shrill whistles from the balcony,
the occasional squeak or blat, the wayward tones.

A brunette, seated, diminutive, cheeks puffed,
delivers deep notes from behind a euphonium.
Clarinetists, serious as ministers, keep the line.
A red-faced boy trumpets a solo to much applause.

Eighth-graders croon "America the Beautiful,"
then choristers in white step through a routine
from *Grease*. It ends with the click, click of sticks
and notes on a bell of an African farewell.

In the parking lot, you walk on air.
Oh spacious skies, oh amber waves of grain.
You are in the mood. Chang chang,
Chang-it-ty chang, shoo-bop, shoo-bop.

CYPRESS TREES

We planted six of them six years ago
on the property line between our house
and the next one before the neighbors built.

Two trees on the uphill side are ten feet tall.
Others, in shale beds, are slow to grow,
though they'll all surpass our expectations—

like our six children. Some of them grew fast,
some at an erratic rate. We raise them the same,
but we cannot control the direction they go.

One cypress has a robin's nest tucked inside,
the bowl of twigs round as the moon and fixed
in the branches. Where did you learn that weave?

The robins come back with their ceramic blue,
the giveaway songs—despite our attentive cat—
and tell us again and again how life will be new.

Branches of lush green-blue push up to the sky,
and our children grow. We do what we think
is right. No one showed us how to build a nest.

WHITE BIRCH IN WINTER

My father and I planted it decades ago—
fledgling landscape at our new house.
Long gone from here and gray at the ears,
I enter the cul-de-sac. The birch smiles
at a pale sky and spreads its silvery wings.

The tree is triple my height, its waist
rivaling mine. Mom and Dad are gone.
Their seven children, married long ago
and away from here, grow a generation
of families and plant their own trees.

Many will come and go in this house
of brick and frame. Children will hang
by their knees from the birch's arms
unaware of the turn and twist of roots
that branch in dark earth as random roads.

The owners would smile at the door
if I were to say, "I grew up in this house.
My father and I planted the trees."
I let go, round the womb of the circle
and mouth the names of old neighbors.

INTERPRETING BLURS

The optometrist says
deciding to wear glasses
will make you lose your ability
to interpret blurs. This may be true
but you remember your first pair of glasses
how the crowds at the mall
suddenly were human, their faces clear
how you could read street signs
from your car. You got used to them
and they gave that look of erudition.

"How far can the eye see?"
you ask the optometrist.
He says there's really no limit
to how far the eye can see.
He relates a tale about Chuck Yeager
who, as a youth, developed a keen eye
for distance when his West Virginia mother
gave him three bullets
and told him to bring home three squirrels
for supper. You imagine Chuck Yeager
up there in the infinite sky
leveling off after a series of barrel rolls
laying his hawkish eye on the trail
of a field mouse.

You're happy to see with corrected vision
and you'll live with bifocals, considering

the alternatives. Miracle lenses. Geneticists map
the tiniest genes. On mountain tops,
sleek telescopes look far into the universe.
We are all blind, Tiresias.

BURNING BUSH

Last week, outside the back windows,
beside the pair of walnut trees, in late fall,
our burning bush blazed crimson.

A month ago, its blue-green, elliptical leaves
shared the sun with four-petal purple flowers.
Then, along with luminous, drooping leaves,

seed pods hung open from long stems—
from dehiscence—the opening of mature fruit
to release their contents. Their inner lives wide open.

Scarlet seeds and leaves from this four-foot shrub
made a Sinai of the woods in our back yard.
"Moses, Moses . . . put off thy shoes from off thy feet."

The fire is gone, the red and green branches bare.
Yet this bush, the shape of a vase, is again ablaze.
My wife has strung the branches with lights.

A wind picks up, twirls leaves in the yard.
We do not speak of our desire for a promised land.
Yet the fire burns low within us, our hearts wide open.

SOCIAL STUDIES

This on my son's history homework: "Balboa
and his men marched across the Isthmus of Panama
and discovered the Pacific Ocean."

Balboa could not think he was the first one. Surely,
the trilobite, Paleozoic pioneer, had cut paths
into the wet sand, had felt the foam, the cold spray.

And the many genial natives, sure of the surprise
they would see on the Conquistadors' faces,
had been raised on tales of their ancestors in awe

at the water's edge, prostrate before their gods,
praying for blessings as they pushed off their boats
into the lure of the wide, relentless sea.

The Europeans, clanking in armor, could clearly see
the significance, the breathtaking sky at the blue edge
of the shimmering waves, the route to gold and spices,

and easily waved off the bronze and smiling women,
the children who ran alongside, anxious for adventure,
and possessed the land for Ferdinand and Church.

Gone with your head went the glitter of fame, Balboa,
yet none can escape the quest. We press toward the light,
keeping our backs to a past where pterodactyls reign.

LIGHTHOUSE

for Richard

For thou hast delivered my soul from death:
wilt not thou deliver my feet from falling,
that I may walk before God in the light of the living?

PSALM 56:13 (KJV)

I stop and raise the lantern's winded wick,
to keep alive its flicker in the spray—
a firefly in fog that's fast and thick—
and push along the cold and moonless way.
My footsteps form in sand along a shore
that cannot keep the prints. They join the sighs
of countless waves that enter with a roar,
but go the way of those we eulogize.
I listen as the crashing carves the sand
while shrouding with a palm my little spark
and know the sea will slowly take the land,
and know the sun cannot outlast the dark.
But up ahead, a cylinder of light
cuts through the pall and sweeps the sky, the night.

COMPOST

Flies buzz in lazy squadrons
over chicken wire borders
to watermelon runways
amid columns of bacterial smoke.
Potatoes ooze between gap-toothed
corn cobs and festering husks.
Maggots squirm in ripe manure
that steams in shovelfuls
from a bed of broccoli stalks,
egg shells, and pea pods.
Oh the stench that rises to heaven
from our collected garbage.
Yet in these putrid heaps
are the makings for harvest.
Lord, my wrongs rankle in me.
My soil is rich for planting.

MATH HOMEWORK

for Abigail

It's the same routine as last night. She hates math,
hates her life, doesn't understand why a seventh grader
needs to know factor trees, how to multiply
negative integers, convert fractions to decimals,
follow the order of operations. Her grade
is in the cellar.

"Do you have graph paper and a pencil?" I ask.
Tonight we divide fractions, multiply by reciprocals.
She groans. "Daddy, please don't drag this out.
I don't want to spend all night on this."
"Math requires building on a foundation," I tell her.
"If you don't get step one, you can't go to step two."
She knows I am going to drag this out, hates her life.

I lose patience and yell when she counts on her fingers,
when she fails to grasp shortcuts, when she stops
to read a nail polish label. Tears drop on her paper.
She erases everything, tries to erase this night,
her experience with math. She looks through tears
and believes she will never get this.

I remember Algebra, how 2x = 6 eluded me,
How $\pi r2$ stood between me and a bright future,
how, for the first time in my life, I was a caged animal,
how I wished Mrs. Miller could explain what she meant
by "solve for x" or "dividing both sides of the equation

by the same number does not change the value of the sides,"
how I came to believe "lowest common denominator"
meant pumping gas for the rest of my life.

"You've got to stick with it, honey," I say.
"Math wasn't easy for me either, but I stuck with it,
and once it finally clicked, I really started to like math."
I don't tell her it started to click when I was forty-three.

When she gets it, she lights up,
says she can solve the rest without my help.
After her shower, she hugs and thanks me.
I squeeze her and take it one day at a time, knowing
how little of what I tell her I can prove.

PAINTINGS

In the basement of my father's house,
in a corner by the fuse box, enshrouded
by spider webs, is a cabinet of oil paintings
dating from his years in art school.

On a visit to this house where I had grown,
I creaked the cabinet door back till a dusty beam
from an overhead bulb discovered inhabitants:
yellowed sketches, portraits lying in state.

Bullet lines from a bolt-action .22 were etched
at angles across the oils. My brother and I
had practiced on beer cans, had shot the life
from magazine ads tacked on the cabinet door.

A Catholic priest was scarred by a white trail
across his cassock. The bullet had grazed
his writing desk, clipped the quill of his pen,
then had skimmed into the basement wall.

In an early portrait of my mother,
a girlish brunette smiled, her head turned
a shade to the side. Her husband had caught
the long hair in mid-swing and the happy eyes.

Brilliant, open lips had endured the years
entombed in the dark. Golden shadows
enriched the high cheeks on the young face
and the glow of the low-necked red dress.

I returned again to darkness the old work,
mounted the stairs, putting tombs from my head.
In the upstairs hall, I stopped to view
a full-length portrait of her later years.

Short hair curled in around brown eyes sobered
by children and an artist. The disciplined shape
and strong face were a lady determined,
standing fast against my adolescent blood.

Now, long after she is gone, her pigments
and hues continue to color my mind.
When I open my mouth to teach my children,
it is she who speaks.

PARALLEL PARKING IN DECEMBER

for Meredith

She is determined to master this,
to take the driving test next week.
Her reasons are ambiguous. Sharing
this grown-up skill brings her closer to us,
yet she feels free to slam the door,
to mutter how stupid and selfish we are,
to leave us behind, to take wing.

It's freezing. I stand in overcoat and gloves
near two plastic, oversized trash cans
I've set up as markers. My toes are ice cubes.
She practices backing with "S" turns
between the cans in the used car
we bought for her. She glowers at me
when I say she is about to climb the curb.

Some of her friends failed on their first try.
This is our only chance to practice
before heavy snow forecast for this evening.
The trees around our house are bare,
their limbs black and gray stick figures
against a white sheet of sky.

Canada geese overhead fly in a curving string.
Their honking gets louder and brings life
to the blank sky, then trails off as they move
over the trees and away from us.

Parallel Parking in December

I turn back at the honking
of my daughter's car. In her anxious face,
I see she's struggling, trying to read in mine
whether I think she's close enough
or too far away.

FORENSICS

It's early spring on this backwoods route
and morning. The sun, a splintered halo, splays
through leafless branches. A red-tailed hawk,
atop a pine, patient for a kill, surveys the land,
in command of the cars on this winding road.

The office is distant, the drive a daily routine.
Ahead, crows scatter from the red-pink carcass
of a skunk. The air for half a mile smells of panic
and death. The enduring evergreens along the road
offset the bleached and ghostly trunks of sycamores.

On the car radio, a newscaster describes
the ongoing abduction trial of a man accused
of molesting a five-year old girl and killing her.
DNA evidence in his car is undoubtedly hers—
taken from the stains of her teardrops.

In grass just turning green, animal skeletons cast off
sunlight. Ahead, a whorl of starlings circles the sky.
As I round a curve, a huddle of vultures, big
as linebackers, picks clean the bones of a deer. One,
disturbed, sidesteps the corpse and throws me a red stare.

EX CATHEDRA

The sodden straps are hot against my wrists,
and as my bleeding ankles chafe their stays,
my twitching muscles reach and twist for ways
to fight the surge that petrifies my fists.
The bowl-shaped crown that clamps my jerking head
rings with waves that jolt the chair and split
my shocking teeth, and through the smoke I spit
a poisoned hiss at you who want me dead.
Come, you jurors straining for the thrill,
enjoy the burning off of sewage found
unworthy of your pious sense of smell.
The thoughts I wish you as a slide to hell
stink with what your putrid hearts impound
and what the volts now make my sphincter spill.

DURING A SERMON I THINK OF EINSTEIN'S THEORY ON THE SPEED OF GRAVITY

Krakatoa, misfit in my theology
what of those on their knees praying,
lovers in the throes of a hot kiss
then boom! the island is gone—
no final trumpet, no white horse and rider.
And the wars, what of mothers
nursing their young, nurturing sons
for the front lines of Gaul, the trenches of Ypres,
the unsuspecting daughters of Nanking,
the men in Rwanda working out their borders
with machetes, hacking out their differences?
And in the Fertile Crescent, what offspring,
its head crowning, is trying to be born?

But a universe without the sun—
what irony after all those years it took
to apologize to Galileo, all those heretics,
their heads shaking with disbelief, burned
at the stake. Should the sun suddenly disappear
along with its gravitational force,
and you work some basic calculations
figuring the speed of gravity
is say 1.06 times the speed of light,
and figuring the eight minutes or so
it will take for the last rays of the sun to reach us,
will we begin to spin before the lights go out?

All those Paternosters,
all those prayers rising as incense.
St. Paul, in your scourging, your being left for dead,
what do we make of this? Plato, should we assume
what we see are shadows on the wall
of a cosmic cave? What will we do
with all of these images: the crescent moon,
the bands of orange sky at night,
the morning glory turning its face
to the first light, and the hummingbird
that seems forever in flight?

FOR JUDY ON THE DEATH
OF HER MOTHER

Days of visitation held endless
prayers. As she lay there
in the dark hours, not remembering,
"Maranatha," you murmured,
and remembered the simple hours
you shared, mother and daughter knitting
yourselves together, comparing
childbirths, what to say to a daughter
who says she can make her own
decisions, about how to shore up
your emotions when decisions
must be made alone.
And here, in the final hour,
when prayers are finished,
when the need to remember
falls from mother to daughter,
the waiting is over, yet cut
by this two-edged sword we still
are waiting. In my front yard, irises
push green blades from frozen ground.

ABISHAG

Abishag the Shunammite
kept King David warm at night.
She lay along his aged length
to rekindle embers of his strength.
Cold in body, old David burned
beside his lovely maid and yearned
for Goliath days, the fame of youth
the ruddy face, forsooth, forsooth.

But son Adonijah wanted her
to be his wife. With heart astir
he asked Bathsheba to make it so.
But Solomon said no—oh no—
and put his aspiring brother to death
and wanted her with his hot breath
as when Uriah was put to the test
by David once. You know the rest.

JEALOUSY AND ENVY

Though different fires, they'll burn a heart in two,
and either one can raze a house the same,
yet desire burned will purge the Cain from you.

It could be young lovers stuck together with glue,
the guy who gets the girl or finds the fame.
Though different fires, they'll burn a heart in two.

Jealousy takes three, but envy a two-toned hue.
To thwart a rival in love is a three-way game,
yet desire burned will purge the Cain from you.

Clutching for another's wife or things, a venue
worn and soiled, will end in shame and blame.
Though different fires, they'll burn a heart in two.

Regret and self-pity tighten like a thumb screw.
You missed the chance, the job, the coveted name,
yet desire burned will purge the Cain from you.

We are Cain and Abel with a split-eyed view
with murder in our hearts and longings aflame.
Though different fires, they'll burn a heart in two,
yet desire burned will purge the Cain from you.

FOR THE MEMORY OF GREG BENDER

(Who Died in a Car Crash)
(1960–1984)

I was the older guy down the street
who used the side yard for football,
organizing my younger brothers
into a blocking machine.

In those fall afternoons
before the ground got too hard
to fall on, Greg was there
with blue eyes and blond hair
looking kinder than any lineman.

Though heavy for his eleven years,
he thought himself too clumsy
for football. But we showed him
how his size, in motion,
could carom a boy to the grass
to consider for a time
how opposing bodies meet and repel.

Newly married, but in a fight
he could not block against,
he got behind the wheel one night
needing strategies
we'd never diagrammed in dirt.

LAZARUS

for Mike

"Lord, if thou hadst been here, my brother had not died."

JOHN 11:21 (KJV)

I.

When Jesus finally showed up in Bethany
Martha was waiting outside, mad as Gehenna.
Why the extra two days? Yet, she still believed in him,
knew he could raise up her brother on the last day.
But no one grasped his intent, his lesson of great love.

Even Thomas had reasoned that being stoned to death
was likely, so they might as well all go with him.
And he'd told them Lazarus was sleeping. Yes, dead,
but there was a plan for glory, of resurrection and life.
Four days in the grave. Necrotic flesh. What a stink.

Lazarus walked out bound hand and foot in grave clothes
in response to a Christ who'd wept. The cave was cool,
sure, and they'd prepped him with oils and spices,
but you think of the oxygen-starved brain cells,
the flattened lung bellows, the puddled organ blood.

LAZARUS

II.

It's Holy Week. Today, I visited a friend in hospice care
at home with his octogenarian parents. In Vietnam,
he'd been built like Schwarzenegger. The fruits
of Agent Orange have blossomed in his yellow body.
He believes he will one day understand God's plan.

For now, he's a Marine: suit up, show up, and shut up.
He's pale, thin, and on his back. The huge biceps
are gone, shriveled as old wineskins. At his request,
every few minutes, I repositioned his aching leg.
He's recorded a song: "How far are you willing to go?"

In forty minutes, he was tired, so I rose to leave.
We shook hands. He did not let go. I held his bony hand,
once hard and fierce as that on axe-wielding Ajax,
and received his blessing. Outside, rows of pear trees
were alive with white flowers. Lazarus, come forth.

EXPLAINING SANTA

Tell all the truth, but tell it slant—
Success in Circuit lies
Too bright for our infirm Delight
The Truth's superb surprise
As Lightning to the Children eased
With explanation kind
The Truth must dazzle gradually
Or every man be blind

—EMILY DICKINSON

I.

My son demands the truth. He's only eight,
but suspects a serious flaw in my universe.
He wants to know if Santa is real. He's irate

from what his sister said. I can't reverse
what's done—that Santa's a lie—yet I'm mute
and know whatever I say will make things worse.

My daughter cannot bear a lie. She's astute
at fourteen, but doubts there is a God.
Her questions make me more resolute

about my beliefs, which she considers odd.
My son threatens to burn my poetry books
to pressure me. I'm now a lightning rod.

I say don't pry into family secrets. He looks,
but doesn't blink. I change my methodology
and say he was lowered to us by shiny hooks

from an alien spacecraft. He grabs my anthology,
so I tell him to ask his sister, the apostate,
who pokes for chinks in my theology.

II.

I do not see a theological checkmate,
yet I cannot easily explain Noah and the ark,
the location of hell, where souls congregate.

Must I say we arose from the accidental dark
as nucleotides churned in a soup? Hidebound
for a million years, upright we now embark

from the womb to raise Cain on this dry ground
as pioneers of selection and raw survival?
Speaking extinction in their ears is unsound.

Must we believe the hominid, on his arrival,
invented himself and truth, beauty, goodness,
and solely through altruism, spares his rival?

And here we have come to godlessness.
Burn the poetry. The archetypes are dead.
Ye meek shall inherit a void and nothingness.

III.

When my tongue sticks as with glue in my head
I do not press on them Adam and Eve, original sin,
nor do I tell them we are but manure in a rose bed.

I speak of trees, the nutrients they take in,
their shelter for birds, of the sequoia's girth,
how leaves emit life-sustaining oxygen,

that animals nest with no instructions on birth,
of the architect hive bee, purveyor of nectars,
that species cling to life and covet this earth.

Outside, the campfire glow of thousands of stars
lights up the night sky. Beside the moon, the flick
of a shooting star guides us to spinning Mars.

Not this close in sixty-thousand years, red as a brick,
in its predictable path, it opens in us a floodgate
as it shuttles by in the slick of its ancient music.

OCTOBER HIKE WITH COPPERHEAD

From the mountain lake, at the dam's overflow,
my grade-school children and I descend a path
beside the waterfall to a creek below.
Recent rains augment the water's crash
down the cliff of granite blocks, grooved
and polished. We push aside needled hemlocks,
then grasp and bend young maples for support.

We cross the creek on mossy rocks to a pond
where dragonflies ripple the opaque surface.
Trees circle its edge and form an umbrella
of shade with iridescent leaves: red maples,
brown oaks, the broad, yellow-green hands
of hickories. Poplar leaves form golden halos
on gray-black trunks speckled white like fawns.

We scale a ledge crowded with mountain laurels,
their leaves waxy green. Gnarled roots grow
from cracks in a shale bed and hug granite slabs
veined with quartz. The children are mountain goats.
A walking stick hitches a ride on my sock.
Mushrooms with inverted, orange caps,
like pancakes, and growing in fairy rings, abound.

At the high side of a cliff along the water's edge,
I stop to examine a chunk of embedded quartz
in the granite ledge. I lean in for a closer look
and see, through bifocals and a foot from my nose,
a copperhead, coiled, still, and facing me.

I awkwardly recoil, nearly fall back
into the ravine, swing my arms and squeal.

The copperhead, sunning in oak leaves, is flat
as a rope faked on a ship's deck. Orange patches,
reddish-brown cross bands, a head smooth and dull
as a worn penny, make it almost invisible. It sleeps.
I imagine myself tumbling down the ravine,
fangs attached to my cheek, the snake whipping
its body to gain a better purchase of flesh.

I feel the venom pumping in my heart
and look for a boulder for the viper's head.
Instead, I show the children the coiled snake
in the rusty leaves and decide I am through
hiking this day. The sleeping snake only does
its snaky thing. With every step I take,
I scan the ground, the leaves, and every stick.

The children, amazed, follow me from the garden.
I look and look, but do not see a flaming sword,
forbidding angels. Overhead, the sun's furnace
hurls the fire of its fusions into the circumference
of space. The tiny arc of fire that coincides
with our hemisphere sheds light and heat,
unmeasured, on good and evil, living and dead.

THE LOVE THAT HANGS OVER US

Because they were hurried
Her feet were loose bound
When she was buried

No time to be married
No dignity found
Because they were hurried

FROM "BOUND FEET" BY PATRICIA CARTER

We walk to heaven, but our feet are bound,
and before we get there, we must be carried.
We struggle on to where we hear the sound.

Long-time lovers know the hallowed ground
where even their deepest thoughts are married.
We walk to heaven, but our feet are bound.

Angels know the language twins have found
for silent speech, their lifetime bond unharried.
We struggle on to where we hear the sound.

We glimpse a light that makes the heart resound,
and, with hope for a place where death is parried,
we walk to heaven, but our feet are bound.

In time, the mind and body will run aground
and, until we founder and our wreck is buried,
we struggle on to where we hear the sound.

Unsteady, we step off this merry-go-round
and fall into our children's arms unhurried.
We walk to heaven, but our feet are bound.
We struggle on to where we hear the sound.

IN WALMART AFTER BEING
PUBLISHED IN THE LOCAL PAPER

My strategy is to avoid eye contact.
You don't want people feeling forced
to say something. In this small town,
it's nearly impossible not to see a neighbor,
someone from school or a soccer team.

I do my shopping, weaving leisurely
through fruits and vegetables, knowing that,
by the pharmacy section, in the news rack,
my poem waits repeatedly and uniform
in a stack of weeklies.

I wait for sliced turkey in the deli line
and assess the shoppers, their potential
for reading an arts section in the paper
and remember that, in the land of the blind,
the one-eyed man is king.

The pretty teen cashier notices my tee shirt.
It's teal and has "Maui" on the chest in gold letters.
"Where's that at?" she says. Another employee
is constructing a sign. "The door is broke," he says
and asks the cashier: "How do you spell 'broke'?"

STRIP CLUB

"Exotic Dancers," the sign says
along this two-lane highway.
"Ladies Welcome." It's unlikely
that ladies crowd the joint, I think,
as I pass by in my car heading home
with grade-schoolers from morning soccer.

"What does 'exotic' mean?"
asks my third-grade son.
His twin sisters, blonde and lovely
in their blue uniforms, hearken.
The children, good readers,
sound out words on passing signs.
The world outside the car is large,
exotic. He repeats the word
and likes the sound of it.

"It means 'unusual' or 'foreign'" I tell him,
and that is all I say. I imagine the grind
of hips, pelvic thrusts, naked flesh
in the swirl of cigar smoke, leering men,
flushed, sweat on their palms,
as tassels rotate on full-moon breasts.
The patrons want no ladies in that dark room.

Women are exotic. This he will learn
on his own—the delicate hand at ease,
extending from the car window ahead of me
at a stop light. The brunette brushing her hair

on the park bench. The lady in a skirt
in the parking lot leaning over groceries.
The looks in women's eyes—blue, green, brown—
their smiles, all beyond knowing, their faces
clear, smooth, their lips so soft.

Powerful, curved legs of an ice skater
in midair, pirouette of a ballerina,
strong and feather light, athletic drive
of a soccer player maneuvering to the goal:
exotic dancers. Brunettes, blondes, redheads—
all of them—loving, compassionate, nurturing—
the ones who lag behind to care for the fallen.

Man, elemental, sees first the curves
and shape of them. Our heads bow
to their plunging necklines,
and we speak to their breasts.
The hues of their skin, their textures,
the perfume of their bodies make men howl.
Why else does a buck stand stupidly
in the road during hunting season?
And why is it pediatricians
call circumcision brain surgery?

Women's minds and tongues sharp as ours,
though they might claim the advantage.
Brute force must yield to their strength.
They are always there forgiving, enduring
the pain of birth, understanding, caressing.
Their laughs, their purring, the resonance
of their voices, all unfathomable.

I could scoop them up into my arms
like flowers. Their faces, thick eyebrows,
high cheeks, curved jaws, slender necks
stun men into silence. Women are beautiful
and everywhere. No man can sound
the depth of them. Take me
to your Maker.

TORTILLA RAP

for Lucy and Lily

I'm getting old and fat, and I sat on my hat.
It's tortilla flat. I throw out these rhymes
to get my twins, *mis gemelas*, to shout,
Yes, Dad, we will. Yo, just chill. We will go
to Spanish Mass, *la Misa en Español*.
We don't get a word, but we will go.
Yo. *Las amo*. Our friends will laugh.
We aren't Spanish, but we will go. Yo.

I tell them *la musica es profonda. El coro
es fantástico.* I will tell them when to kneel,
to cross themselves, to stand or sit. Just feel.
The words will come. Feel the uplift, the Spirit,
the harmony—*el ritual, las oraciones.*
Just take it in *mis niñas, mis inocentes.*
Maybe *mi primera hija* will go and bring
mi nieta, my sweet granddaughter.
Mia Rose. You make me sing.

I pick up my hat. What do you think of that?
With a whap, it's no longer flat. It's on my head
with visor pointing back. My pants are loose
and falling down. My pants are falling down.
I'm strutting my stuff. I'm going to hang tough
and use only a few f-words: *fajitas, frijoles,
muy fecunda, muy fecunda.* Call me *loco*,
but I am calling this a wrap, a tortilla rap
a tortilla rap.

SPEEDBOATING AT DAM 4

Thirty feet behind us, on an inflated raft,
linked by a nylon rope, my son grips hand straps
and hangs on. I'm the spotter. My friend is driving
the center console boat at 3500 RPMs. He swerves,
then looks to see if my son is still on. Dylan,
thirteen, crosses the wake with hair blown back
from a melon face that turns from joy to fear
as he survives the turns, the slapping rides.
He raises a thumb to indicate "Go faster."

I went first on the raft, and, at 4000 RPMs,
when thrown, nearly lost my suit, but for a big toe.
I am content to watch from the boat. I prefer
a slower speed, the propeller's gurgle, the low,
steady growl of the engine. Tall, gray faces of granite
jut out from summer forest growth along the banks
where trees and water find their mutual limits.
A tolerant blue heron, on a storm-downed tree,
at the edge, watches as we speed by.

The line to my son is taut. He wants this
to go on forever. I scan cliffs for an eagle's nest,
follow the green Potomac river's curve, the flow
to the Chesapeake. Down river, storm clouds churn
the northwestern sky. It's nearly dusk.
A sliver of orange peeks through. I check the rope,
which holds, but know one day it will break.
I cannot keep the storm clouds away, but trust
my son will take them on thumbs up.

MERCY

In the foyer, my daughter's high school friend,
a blonde, introduces herself as Portia.

"Someone in the family likes Shakespeare,"
I say. She is puzzled, so I say her name.

"Oh," she says, "my mother named me
after someone in a soap opera." I show clemency,

for I have been forgiven my pound of flesh.
Chloe, our ninety-pound black Lab, dozing, slaps

the mooring line of her tail on the oak floor.
In this large family, she is the only one

who does what I say. Chloe's face tightens
to a fruit bat smile. I fetch her leash.

She bounds, nails clicking across the floor.
My heart swells. I forgive everyone and bless

the neighbor cat that sprayed in my garage,
and whoever called the Homeowners' board

because of my dog's barking at nothing.
How could they know that Chloe, barking upward,

is clearing crows from her airspace? "Come girl,"
I say, "Daddy is taking you for a walk."

REJECTION SLIP

On the evening news, you are watching video
of Saturn's rings streamed in from the orbiter
while you sort through a day of junk mail.
It's then you see it—a wrinkled SASE.

Your name and address, in your own blue pen,
remind you of prisoners told to dig their graves,
then to stand in front of them. And the stamp
you licked, the commemorative Purple Heart.

The SASE holds a sliver of periwinkle paper.
It's a small thing with small type that says little:
"Though your work has been declined by our editors,
we thank you for allowing us to consider it."

You press the SASE in with others on your desk,
in an accordion of envelopes where poems molder.
Like Walt Whitman, you tire of learned astronomers
and go out to look up in perfect silence at the stars.

Yet a friend, an astronomy buff, says, in time
our Sun will go supernova, how it is likely
a comet will slam into us and create a dust cloud
to make the end of dinosaurs seem like child's play.

All it takes is for one editor to sit back breathless
in a swivel chair, giddy as Archimedes, re-reading
your poems and saying, "Eureka!" Please hurry
whoever you are. We are running out of time.

BURNING A TOAD

for Dylan

"Toward misted and ebullient seas
And cooling shore, toward lost Amphibia's emperies.
Day dwindles, drowning, and at length is gone
In the wide and antique eyes, which still appear
To watch, across the castrate lawn,
The haggard daylight steer."

RICHARD WILBUR FROM "DEATH OF A TOAD"

My son is angry at me. I am not a hunter.
He wants to kill deer, see entrails, blood spatter,
be like his friends who hunt with their fathers.
My dad was an artist. He danced the jitterbug.

His dad had been a boxer in Boston.
Tales survive of his rages, of pulling motorists
from cars in traffic and roughing them up.
My son says he can take me with one hand.

It was high school, my friend's back yard.
We smoked non-filtered Camels. Psychedelic.
In the mornings, on the edge of my bed,
I'd hack and hack to jump-start my lungs.

In the dark backyard, all testosteroned up,
I flicked my lighter against Levi jeans
and lit the gas-doused toad. What a riot.
We guffawed as it hopped into the night.

His father threw open the screen door.
His condemnation, the awkwardness, my eyes
averting him—they are with me still. My friend,
high on grass, later died in a motorcycle crash.

No more Camels. Funny how common sense
can seep into a hard head. I breathe clean air
and see that toad crossing the lawn, Elijah,
in his flaming chariot, lighting the way.

NEW TERMS

for Beth

informal lump detection, lumpectomy
pseudolumps, calcifications
dense breasts, nipple discharge
inverted nipples, aspirate
chronic subareolar abscess
intraductal papilloma
atypical lobular hyperplasia
scentimammography
sentinel node biopsy, positive nodes
ductal carcinoma in situ
invasive cancer
intracystic papillary carcinoma
malignant, melanoma
skin-sparing mastectomy
axillary lymph node dissection
drains, fluid collecting
lymphedema
polychemotherapy
chemotherapy-induced nausea
hair loss, dopamine antagonists
chemobrain
breast reconstruction
latissimus flap with silicone implant
reversible menopause, hormone therapy
radiation, skin burn, rib fractures
balloon-delivered intracavitary brachytherapy
neuropathy, metastasis

recurrence, remission
patient's right to know
quality of life, hospice
core biopsy of fibroadenoma
benign, yes, benign

FIBROADENOMA

for Beth

The radiologist rolls the word like music
from her lips. It is likely just that,
a benign tumor in the right, the remaining
breast. She recommends a biopsy
since the left breast, a memory, had nurtured
the invasive, ductal carcinoma. More music.
Wife, mother, caretaker, giver of milk, of life
to our children, is easily shaken by this.

The female breast, center of the universe,
source of the river of life, is taken from within,
brought down by its own hormonal asteroids.
How can a woman marvel again at her body,
its allure, its galactic symmetry, its planetary
pull, when the not knowing has replaced
the expected rising and setting of the sun,
the every-day firmness of her warm breasts?

We schedule a biopsy for the following week.
The wait will be a terror of imaginings, part
of her new life where, even for the most devout,
women review the percentage of recurrence,
how effective the chemo is, chances of survival
for the different stages. You hear clichés,
like "gun shy," or "waiting for the other shoe
to drop." I am here, but this is hers to ingest.

HAIRDO

for Beth

The reddish-brown wigs are of such quality
that no one who does not know her
knows they are wigs.

In the pharmacy drive-through, a lady complimented
the formal, two-toned do. Almost compelled
to set her straight, she said, "Thank you. Thank you."

She is sick and resting in bed. She's got the chemo blues.
She's Mr. Clean with pendant earrings.

The front door opens. The dog wags its tail. The slap
of tail against the oak floor is a clue the visitor is friendly.
Soon, up the stairs, the slow pat, pat, pat of footsteps.

Mr. Clean, eyes closed, speaks up: "Hi, Mom."

"How did you know it was me?"

"The dog's tail wagged."

Her mother rounded the bed. She, still resting,
opened her eyes, then wider, and laughed.
She saw herself in a mirror. Same shiny head,
lovely blue eyes. Her mother stood there grinning—
shaved bald.

"Solidarity, man!" she said.

CHEST PAINS

I'm in the ER in gown and jeans. The curtain
of my cubicle is open. I chat with a young woman
in street clothes sitting on her bed. Her curtain is open.
She has two sons and smiles as she describes them.
One likes football, the other baseball.
She has migraines. She is thinking brain tumor.

I have a persistent pain that feels as if I got punched
in the chest just left of center. I'm thinking
it's from the four feet of snow I shoveled and then,
this spring, from the seven yards of mulch.
I am thinking tumor-wrapped aorta
or peanut-shaped plaque in a coronary artery.

In the ER cubicle across from mine, a surgeon
talks to a man about the softball-sized growth
on the man's inner thigh. The curtain is open.
The surgeon wants to admit him.
The man asks the ER nurse to call his girlfriend
to let her know he won't be coming home tonight.
He wants to go out for a smoke.

He wants me to see the growth on his leg.
I glance at it out of respect.
"It's like a car accident," the ER nurse says,
"where you should, but don't want to, look away."

The man talks about a past heart attack, how,
while pushing a mower, his left side went numb.

CHEST PAINS

"I felt like I had pins and needles in me," he says.
Soon, attendants arrive and roll him away
on his bed with wheels.

After an EKG, a blood test, and chest X-rays,
I learn I have inflamed cartilage where ribs
meet breastbone. I am Paul Bunyan
and embarrassed to be here among the sick.
I drive home repeating the word "costochondritis."

In the kitchen, I empty the dishwasher
and note the marvelous colors and designs on plates,
the glorious curves of goblets, and outside,
on the deck rail, the magnificent music of a wren.
Later, in bed, with my hand, I trace the lovely,
warm, and steady thigh of my sleeping wife.

RADICAL PROSTATECTOMY

It's not brain surgery, but close.
In the recovery room, you wink
at the young RN as she checks placement
of the catheter. You feel sexy.
You push away doubts and the "i" words:
impotence and incontinence.

The surgeon spared the nerves
with the da Vinci® robotic system.
He is confident and expects the pathology
to show negative margins. You dismiss
the other "i" word: incompetence.

Guy friends joke about a future
with diapers. One says it depends.
Your wife says not to worry. After surgery,
at home, you will be pampered.

The surgeon said not to be pessimistic.
Urinary continence will return.
Two weeks after surgery, diapered,
you are feeling pissimistic.

You're on sick leave. At home, robed,
you putter from room to room
and hang the urine bag from bathrobe belt.
It's time to catch up on poetry magazines,
crime-solving shows, the book of *Romans*.

Radical Prostatectomy

Deciding on surgery was tough.
The surgeon said, "You are relatively young.
You have good life expectancy. The cancer
is likely contained in the prostate.
Have the surgery and remove the cancer."

You had read about the prostate—a walnut—
its functions, the interconnectedness
with other manly parts: the interworking
with bladder, urethra, seminal vesicles.
We are marvelously made.

You're thinking of the pragmatic: the wife,
the six kids, the job you need to keep.
Let's get this done. On your shoulder,
though, a voice says "No way. Ignore it.
It's the end of your sex life. Head for Mexico.
Line up the señoritas. Eeyaah."

Here you are, bent over, underwear down,
fitting a pad into your jockeys. You recall years
of watching your wife bent over, pants down,
arranging this and that between her legs.
Bless her and all women,

and bless the anesthesiology team of ladies
in decorative OR caps who explained
that they would be by your side throughout
the surgery, and that yes, stirrups
are part of the procedure. You replied that now
you know how women feel. They said, with a laugh,
"This is our chance to get men back."

The pathology shows negative margins.
You're doing your kegels. Goal one
is to regain continence. Your wife is pampering you.
No one cares if you telecommute in diapers.
You're looking forward to a dinner date,
first blooms on the redbud you planted last year.

GHAZAL FOR JITTERBUG

Father and mother, both long dead tonight,
your unfinished lives fill my head tonight.

A few more years might have worked it out.
I picture you married, not this dread tonight.

I lie sleepless watching your wartime jitterbug,
but the happy family years have fled tonight.

Imagine us all together, you smiling and gray,
our families with us, good things said tonight.

You grew into one for twenty-five years,
but broke apart. I keep my children fed tonight.

I look for chinks in my thirty-year love
and throw a leg across my wife in bed tonight.

JUNCTION

for Corbyn

Day and night, trains rattle by loaded
with cargo and intersect in this rural town.
Plan for delays at crossings. Alongside
the soccer fields, expect a whistle,
a train's thunder, the engineer's wave,
the end of conversation as cars click by.

After a late night at a bar on a Sunday,
a twenty-two-year-old man on foot
met a winter train head on. The engineers
must have gasped at the math
of man against speed and steel.

A man is gone: father of a girl too young
to know. Son, lover, student, agitator,
philosopher, determined to find his own way,
rumbling, confident, down his own tracks.
Even in death, the smirk, that
I-am-smarter-than-the-rest-of-you look.

Hundreds of admirers, family, friends,
the little girl's mother (our daughter),
are smashed by grief. At the gravesite
they stood, huddled, raven black, drained
of tears, hollowed, barren, numb. Shock
keeps everyone moving. It will take years
for these dark wings to unfold.

JUNCTION

At this junction of ending, of starting,
the mourners disperse, return to their cars,
go forward, each in his own direction,
each hauling bags to a future without a son,
a brother, a friend, a lover, a father.

And Mia, at one, her father visible in her face—
a bond for two families—and all of us due
to wake up tomorrow in a world where,
whatever tracks we ride, this man
will be central to the intersecting story,
one filled, like this one, with events no one
could have imagined.

BABY

for Jade

It's a natural process, yes,
the body's way to say no
to the embryo, the little one
clinging to the womb
the fragile, developing form,
baby, the Mr. or Mrs. whoever
you were going to be
had not the body said no,
something is amiss, this birth
will not happen, you month old,
fledgling child, you echo
of the heartbeat, the desire
of your mother, her womb
the home, the percolator,
the starting place of the life
you did not grow into, you
intricate DNA, the intertwining
of your parents, you, longed for,
the light in your mother's eyes,
you, who cannot be carried,
loved one, spark of life,
stopped, discharged, free to go,
no room at the inn, denied
the parting labial entry
into the world, miscarriage
of justice, we will never
forget you.

HAIRCUT

Warm and shirtless before the wood stove,
with a broom, I sweep hair my wife trimmed
from my head with clippers, scissors, and comb.

I fetch the dustpan. Strands of gray mingle
with light browns that lived on my head.
I've washed and combed and slept in that hair.

Iron hinges creak on the wood stove door.
A lasso of flames swirls out from the red oak.
I throw in hair from the dustpan and shrink
from the incinerating blast, the flare.

The smell conjures up my arm hairs aflame
as a boy, when I learned the quick way
to start a fire by spraying lighter fluid from a can.

You cope with the smell by breathing shallow
through your mouth, saving your nose. Do it enough,
I suppose, and you get used to the bad air.

I think of barbers at Buchenwald, tired
of sweeping hair—the browns, the grays, the dark curls—
who must have said, as the war droned on,
you see one head, you've seen them all.

SWING

"When I beheld our sons
as, in the way of things, they will not be again
though even years from now their hair may lift
a little in the breeze, as if they stood
somewhere along the way from us,
poised for a steep return."

HENRY TAYLOR FROM "AT THE SWINGS"

Mia Rose, one, says "Ming, Ming,"
so I lead her to the black cherry tree
where her swing hangs from two ends
of a cable wrapped above and around
the diagonal trunk. An intersecting branch
grows straight up.

The tree escaped the smoking whine
of my chain saw. At best, its trunk points
to the sky at forty-five degrees. It's perfect
for the swing, and, like me, has survived
in a life that left the expected path
and has thrashed along a diagonal.

Strapped in and smiling, Mia flies
to the edge of the woods. As she returns,
I push her again, and say, "go!" She squeals.

Our daughter's daughter brings joy to all
who meet her. Exuberant cackles in our home

bring life where death reigned some months ago.
She has no sense of her dead father and does not ask
of him. Her smiling face is a duplicate of his.

She revels in the rush of air, the forth and back
on the wires. We will continue to push her,
to receive her into our arms—as does the other pair
of grieving grandparents—while our daughter,
twenty-two, adjusts to tragedy.

We push our own children out and hope
they will fly, but believe they will remain
in a trajectory that swings them back to us.
We interlock with Mia's tiny arms and press
to ourselves her happiness aware she has,
by merely being here, awakened in us this wonder.

WHY I LIKE THE VILLANELLE

for John Case

This rustic, country song, deep as a well,
thrives despite the claims that rhyme is dead,
for beating hearts can never say farewell.

Yes, repeated lines are hard to sell,
but artfully done can rise like a loaf of bread,
this rustic, country song, deep as a well.

One can hear the ocean in a shell
and feel the waves above an oyster bed,
for beating hearts can never say farewell.

It's fair to say it's tough to write them well,
but souls need rhythmic music to keep them fed,
this rustic, country song, deep as a well.

You know it works if you feel, inside, a gazelle
that leaps, your hair just standing on your head,
for beating hearts can never say farewell.

They're wrong who say they hear a funeral bell.
They're drawn to it with a sing-songy dread—
this rustic, country song, deep as a well—
for beating hearts can never say farewell.

A CHIPMUNK IN THE CAT'S MOUTH

The others warned me, told me to look for her,
but I was enthralled in seed by the feeder,
dancing with joy in the breeze and sun.
Stop it; that hurts. She's got my neck;
damn those teeth.

From what they say, she will drop me,
give me a chance, but it's rare to get away.
I've heard of one miracle. The homeowner
scolded the cat, and she dropped her prize.
If you play dead, you could surprise her
and bolt for a tree or the space
under the base of the basketball hoop.

Is it the white stripes up the back
that lead her to us? The contrast of stripes
on the lush, brown fur has been our trademark,
and our cuteness, our round eyes
and the way we wiggle our whiskers. Such beauty,
such intricate complexity in our beings
to go down ignominiously into the crunch, crunch
of her molars.

I don't blame the cat. She's an awesome hunter.
Yes, I've seen her pull a dove from the bird bath,
and she hauled a rabbit home headless
and laid it on the back deck. Yes, and squirrels.
One looked garroted, bloody at the neck.
Elders say this is the way of it. We are tried here,

then we go to a better place. Stop it, damn you.
Loosen up on the needle points.

My God. She dropped me. I play dead now,
hope for a chance to run. I have kids to feed,
a wife who will be burdened. I must survive.
Sure, I've done bad things. I am sorry for them.
I'd like another chance. Here comes the paw.

FLYING BACK EAST FROM LAS VEGAS

This was a winter business trip. You are not a gambler.
You have been surprised enough: the blinking lights,
the ubiquity and hum of slot machines, the blackjack tables,
the half-naked woman in the elevator. Bleary-eyed visitors
from anywhere robbed by the one-armed bandit,
yet wandering around for one more try. Serving girls
strung tight as rigging and projecting cleavages
both fore and aft. Billboards that wink
and invite you to lose more than your money.

It came to this after the view from thirty-thousand feet where,
like a schoolboy, you'd pressed your face to the glass
and lost your breath at the painted flatlands and plateaus,
the purple mountains of late afternoon, the Grand Canyon—
the million acres plowed by Babe the blue ox—
where you'd held back, at seeing the canyon sides, the urge
to give praise—the layer cakes of reds and tans stacked by eons
of geologic time—the buttes and spires, desolate, beautiful,
where the Colorado swells, cuts a blind path through rock.

Behind the lights, the strip, the fantasies of the fertile valley
is this heroic effort of the best minds, the fattest wallets:
to etch a place into this nowhere in the middle of nothing
but sand, wind, distant mountains, the bleakness
of billions of years on a landscape hospitable as Mars.
At night, satellites can see the human glow,
the high-watt bulb. And there the line drawn in the sand:
the clubs, the foreverness of booze, of showtime,
the fluorescent stars—a glittering confusion of tongues.

You got a window seat. You wait for the Airbus to bank
to McCarran Airport where you were amazed to see,
as you passed disheveled and shoeless through the gate,
more slot machines—a last watering hole for some,
a chance to win back the mortgage for others.
The plane dips, and you see the architectural wonders
in concrete and glass—monuments to the unlucky.
You are tongue-tied. Soon, below, the Colorado flows.
You strain to know the source of this earth's deep gash.

MAPLE SYRUPING

A sugar maple needs a crown of branches,
a trunk at least eleven inches thick, and time
to let the thin sap rise to a pulsing flow
that lasts for several weeks. The maple
will accept the loss if sap the workers gather
is from straight trees with healthy roots.

The clear sap pumps from the roots
and moves to the tops of branches
from late January to mid-April. To gather,
wait for days freezing or above and time
to drill in the tree base when the maple,
a thawing river, is in its maximum flow.

Syrupers drill a half-inch hole for the flow
three inches deep a few feet from the roots,
then drive a metal spout into the maple.
A bucket hangs on the spout, which branches
to a hook. A trickle means, in a few days' time,
a bucketload will be ready to gather.

Buckets on spouts guide collectors who gather
at tree bases and tip the buckets to let sap flow
into hand-held buckets. Once they're full, it's time
for the tractor-pulled gathering tank, which roots
its way in snow between holly trees or branches
of spruce and hemlock or a low-hanging maple.

Maple Syruping

The sugar house, a simple shed of maple
and rough pine, is where workers gather
to boil down the yield. The crew branches
into teams to split wood and lets the sap flow
by electric pump to a holding tank. A crew roots
twigs and bugs from the frothy tank at this time.

The firebox, hot with pine, burns up the time
it takes the sap to fill evaporators above. The maple,
friend of flapjacks, revives as its sap boils to sugary roots.
Once filtered, it boils again, and amber begins to gather.
Workers use sterilized jars to collect the sweet flow.
A one-quart jar holds the sap of many branches.

It's time to drill the trees when butterflies gather
within you, and the maple sap of your blood begins to flow
from its roots and shoots to the tips of your branches.

JUNK DRAWERS

A pair of them side by side in the kitchen island.
You need a clothes pin to clamp a bag of tortilla
chips. Task one: untangle or cut the Gordian knot
of cell-phone-charger wires, yellow and red yarn,
blue thread, white shoelace, green extension cord,
gift ribbon, brown packaging string. (Some day.)
Underneath, AAA batteries lie scattered. Magic
markers. Colored pencils everywhere—long and
short, sharp and dull. A history of school projects
peeks out. The crayons, matches, scissors, paper
clips of our lives are here quiet, but alive. Trash
bag ties, a stapler. Candles can light the way. The
CDs and lollipops of our days, the nights of dog
brush, ruler, comb, dice, the bag of squash seed.
Listen as the day-to-day speaks here the language
of glue sticks, pens, plastic pears, dominoes, and
phone books. Here's the missing Christmas tree
ornament. Embrace your life. Celebrate it in note
pads, sparklers, crazy glue, flashlight, flower food,
plastic tape, green rubber bands. Ah, a clothes pin.

WORSHIP

On my knees, I raise inquiring eyes,
and, with thanksgiving, lift obedient hands
and praise you with the miracle of my tongue.
You are my breath, the beat of my diesel heart,
yet unbelief keeps buzzing in my ears.
I want to know you with my reasoning mind.

Uncertainty erodes my steadfast mind
and, like my namesake, want to see with my eyes
that you are there—real—with listening ears
(all I have are metaphors) and hands
that pull us daily to your loving heart
and lips that speak to us in a common tongue.

I steer to you with the rudder of my tongue
chanting words of faith, but in my mind
are the mathematics of death. My heart
longs for a world at peace, yet with my eyes
I see wars without end and blood on men's hands.
The thunder of missiles and bombs punctures our ears.

Millennia of prayers meant for your ears
echo in ether from every nation and tongue.
We did not build this universe with our hands,
but are stranded here—with a logical mind—
our bodies kin to stars and flowers, our eyes
scanning heaven as searchlights of the heart.

WORSHIP

Nietzsche's words will not resound in my heart,
and Truth in lower case just hurts my ears.
I take the measure of science with critical eyes,
accept its laws, yet cannot put to tongue
the cosmological awe that fills my mind.
The majesty just pushes up my hands.

What complexity of choice is in our hands,
the myriad paths that open from the heart.
The genetic pool of language in the mind
is ours to frame as music to others' ears,
ours to dictate life or death with the tongue,
ours to speak forgiveness with our eyes.

My eyes drink in the sunrise. I raise my hands,
yet my tongue sings of a hole in my heart.
Oh, touch my ears and heal my double mind.

I DO

for Lib

At the altar, you're in love, stricken, buoyed on clouds
imagining the years together living your dreams,
buying your own house, raising kids, watching them excel.

"Love and cherish" bubbles up from inside. "For richer
or for poorer" sounds like music. You are sure
you can do this. How did you ever meet this person?

You don't think forty years ahead after that fervent "I do."
Your loved one is lying in bed terminally ill. Words
have ceased. You're changing diapers, counting out pills,
collecting soiled linens. Is that hospice at the door?

When you say "I do," you're thinking of the honeymoon,
the hot nights on the beach. "Kiss me, baby."

Maybe it's a natural blindness, a hiding of the grimness
from youth. Who would ever say "I do"
at the inevitable breakdown of body and bones,
the wrinkles, the mind going?

That is you on the bed, in sickness and in health,
forsaking all others. In that face, you see your children,
the ones who comfort you now. You are one flesh.
Yes, of course, I do. I do.

MIA ROSE AT FOUR

She's smarter than I am, and she knows it.
That's OK. I would give my life for her—
inquisitive, cute and lovely granddaughter.

We're heading for church. In the back,
in her car seat, she pushes the button
to lower the window. In front,
at the master control, I push it up.

"It's cold. Leave the window up," I say.
She pushes the button again. I reverse it.
She's giving me that don't-even-think-about-it
look. I push the window lock button.
She concedes, but not quietly.

We are talking about days of the week.
She asks me where Saturday comes from.
"I believe it is named after the planet Saturn."
"Oh, then that means Sunday is named
after the Sun," she says.

"I don't think so, but I will look it up."
At home, I am on dictionary.com. Sunday.
Origin. Latin. *dies solis*: day of the sun.

TEXTING WITH A TEEN

for Dylan

"fu—to erase, to take back, to make into nothing"
—JUDY HALEBSKY FROM "HOW TO FIND A MAN UP TO THE TASK"

I told the poet, after her reading,
"Now I know what my son means
when he texts 'FU' to me." It's tough
to follow the shortcut language of teens.
I am glad to have discovered,
in Japanese symbols, how to relate to my son.

Take last week when I texted him
to mow the lawn. His response—WTF—
made me think he was suggesting a day:
Wednesday, Thursday, or Friday.
I responded: "Today." He said "OMG."
He texted that he was playing X-Box.

Years ago, I lost my first son
to real-time, online war games.
We'd had a few years of chess,
but my level of commitment waned
when we moved to hand-held controllers.

I asked son number two when he would be done
on X-Box. "IDK," he said. "Mow before dark,"

I said. He texted "whatever," and probably did it
without looking at the keys on his cell phone.

My sons play war games together across the world.
The first one, a sailor, is in Tokyo on a ship.
Son two is in our basement in West Virginia.
They use headphones and converse
while they massacre each other's armies
in an Internet war room on X-Box.

IDK, maybe I need to loosen up. As a kid,
I'd stand up plastic soldiers and shoot them down
with rubber bands. The thrill was there,
but not the technology. No, I think it's too late
to join that fight. Chess, anyone?

HEART ROCK

We're near the lifeguard chair
on a towel thirty feet from the ocean
reading our books. The rain stopped.
We'd shielded ourselves with a boogie board
during the downpour. Now, in hot sun again,
we've dried out. We spray on the white lather.

Our kids aren't here. We can't remember
being alone without them. Waves wash in
with a regular rhythm. The ocean speaks,
undisturbed, with its expected crash and fizz.
We've been together for thirty-plus years,
and, like the waves, we will carry on,
raise our kids, be a steady hum in their lives.

The water was cold, even in July.
It took bravery to go in. But here
we are celebrating her birthday. Knowing
she wanted me to go in, I did, despite the shock.
You back into the waves to soften the blows.

The beach was clear, the sand trodden
by millions of people. Shells were scarce.
Yet, she found a dark stone, heart shaped,
honed for centuries. It is a birthday gift
from the ocean.

It says, "Take my weathered shape." You know
the effects of years, how they can break you,

but you have endured the struggles, the trials
of children, of illness, of financial horrors.
You are loved by everyone you know, by the sand
you walk on, by this love-shaped stone, by me.

SPHYGMOMANOMETER

Take the word in parts: sphyg
is like sphinx without the inx.
Sphygmos: Greek for pulse.
Mano-: denotes gas or vapor.
Meter: an instrument for measuring.
Manometer: a pressure or vacuum gauge.
Sphygmomanometer: an instrument
used to measure blood pressure.
Understanding the pulse is complicated.
Hippocrates knew that, and Galen.

With the rubber cuff wrapped around
your upper arm, use the rubber bulb
attached by tube to inflate the cuff
until the pressure gauge registers
two hundred millimeters of mercury.
The brachial artery will have collapsed.
Then, with the stethoscope applied
to the same artery, below the cuff,
slowly release the pressure.
The blood will rush back, splashing
into the artery, powered by diesel-throbs
from the contracted heart.
Check the pressure gauge and record
when the thumps begin.
As the artery fills, and the heart relaxes,
record the stoppage of sound.

SPHYGMOMANOMETER

You listen to the life-surge returning,
as it must, until the glub-glub
of the blood subsides
into the muffled beats of a bass drum
following the creaks of a carriage
conveying a body along.
Close your ears to the echoes
of the returning pulse rumbling
with a vague thunder of uncertainty
and avoid the ridding fears
the Thebans knew, helpless
before the immovable face of the sphinx.

SUNSET ON BLUE RIDGE

You can tell me that the red wisps of cloud,
arms and legs spread-eagled across the sky
from a fiery torso, are not Spiderman,
that the silky strands are not his hands,

that the orange trails leading off to the edge
of the purple mountains were not spun by him,
that the pink cotton balls he lassos in the range
of baby blue are merely cumulus clouds,

water drops, particles of dust, pollution,
that his red arms and legs are merely crystals
of light-reflecting ice, cirrus clouds,
reaching aimlessly across an empty sky to nowhere,

that the black anvil riding in from the west
across the Blue Ridge this steamy afternoon,
does not bring Venom, his nemesis,
for the inevitable clash. You can say it is merely

cooled, expanding air, the upward rush of wind,
a towering cumulonimbus, heaped up
and meaningless, spilling its flash and flood
at random on an uncomprehending earth,

that superheroes and villains do not clash,
that Zeus and Hephaestus with their fiery craft
are mere vapors in the summer sky, that Moses
and the pillar of cloud and pillar of fire are tales

old men tell to hope for meaning. I grasp
for Occam's razor, yet hold my free hand
outstretched high in the sky, like Adam,
and feel for the electric finger's charge.

STRAWBERRIES

for Melanie

Oh champion fruit, red and juicy and sweet,
I see a hint of smile in your seeded face.
You seem to know how good you are to eat.

With regal crown of leafy green, you beat
the odds of slugs and snails and found your place,
oh champion fruit, red and juicy and sweet.

The Romans knew your silent gift to treat
depressed and anxious souls with your embrace.
You seem to know how good you are to eat:

your antioxidants, a heart's receipt
for health, the anti-cancer touch of grace,
oh champion fruit, red and juicy and sweet.

The pies and shakes, the jams and cakes that greet
our hungry eyes and tastes we can't erase.
You seem to know how good you are to eat.

How complicated nature is, replete
with cosmological threads that interlace.
Oh champion fruit, red and juicy and sweet,
you seem to know how good you are to eat.

BEAUTY

for David Craig

Go away. I know you are out there lurking,
MR. DEATH.

The name, Raquel Welch, means nothing
to my son, twenty-two. Has no clue, nor does
he care who she is. Perhaps I should ask him
who the women are that inspire him,
that take his breath away.

Yes, Solomon, we know all is vanity,
that we are as blades of grass, but how can one
ever let go of Sophia Loren, Gina Lollobrigida,
Ann-Margaret, Barbara Eden, Elizabeth Taylor,
Brigitte Bardot, and Ingrid Bergman?

We've been at this for a long time.
Look at the luscious and ancient lines
in *Song of Songs* where the couple savors
the fruit and basks in the sun and petals
of love making.

Where are they now, those lovelies
from generations past? Yes, we know
the resounding hum of dust to dust.
Oh you loved ones—family and friends, relatives,
and the uncountable beauties—we miss you.

HORNET NEST

for Ryan

My college-aged son and I are
two bucks. Our chests touching, we
catch our horns on chandeliers, in coat hangers.
When I'm home, he stays clear of my grazing area.
When I'm gone, he becomes me. When we talk, my
temples sting. Once, on the Appalachian Trail, we agreed.
He was ten. We hiked a lot then—with rock hammers. We
picked up quartz or granite from the trail, chipped it, put
samples in our knapsacks. Keeping up meant following
him across boulders, into caves, to side paths, always
behind, hearing—never seeing—frogs plopping
into ponds, startled turkeys flapping for takeoff,
the thrash of leaves as foxes ran, the shrieks of
pileated woodpeckers. That one time, he had
stopped to wait near a tree-hung hornet nest.
Big as an urn, it was a perfect target. Though
stung by conscience, I seized a chunk of
quartz, threw it, but missed wide. My son,
the accomplice, chipped granite into
throwable pieces. The hornets, at
every hit, clouded the sky. We
kept it up, my son seeing,
at last, his father. The
hornets, unimpressed,
swore: "Once you
lock on, sting
the hell out
of them."

SALVAGE YARD

You're there looking for used parts
for your daughter's car. She'd backed up,
turned, hit a fence post, broke the left front
lights and pulled off the bumper.

You park next to a red Ford pickup truck.
On its rear window, passenger side,
a Rebel flag waves at you. Below it,
it says "If you don't know what this is,
you need to be educated."
On the driver's side is a strong affirmation
of the Second Amendment.

They have the parts. While the guy walks
to the yard filled with half-eaten vehicles,
you approach the office window.
"Do you have a bathroom here?"
The guy inside says, "What do you need to do?"
"Number 1."
"Just go out there between some cars," he says.
"That's what we normally do."

You thank him, turn, and walk away.
You're standing between a fender-less Chevy
and looking into the bed of a Dodge pickup.

The guy is back with the parts: two light fixtures.
You've got the bolts and washers to re-mount

the bumper. You head for home to fix the car and wonder how the guy answers people who say "Number 2."

MAMA

Our household of six kids has included dogs,
cats, rabbits, goldfish, a cockatiel, an iguana,
hamsters, and guinea pigs. The kids are grown,

but we still have a dog, Samson (a Great Pyrenees—
aka polar bear), two cats, Eennie and Sunny, and two
guinea pigs. Our twin daughters got the guineas,

Hot Chocolate and Cookie. We will never be bored.
The kids, like the animals, want Mama. Dad is here,
but not the first choice for parental consultation.

The animals follow Mama around and call for her.
When she enters the bedroom—yes, the guineas
are in our room—they start a conversation:

"Whoeep whoeep. Where have you been all day?
We need you." Samson, huge, white and hairy,
sits on half of Mama's chaise lounge with her

for a head rub. His fellow dogs would mock him.
The two cats wait for their turns to be with Mama.
Even the flowers wave to her.

MOBY DICK

My granddaughter enters the study and reviews
some books on the shelves. She is eight and says,
"That book has a cuss word in its title."

I will steer her thinking and explain the importance
of Melville's bringing into the first sentence
the split nations of Abraham, the thousands of years
where nations have clashed in wars with their neighbors.
"Call me Ishmael."

She needs to know the story of Sarah and Hagar, how Isaac
got the throne, how Hagar and Ishmael were sent away.
She needs to hear the sounds of Rachel weeping
for her children and to understand what drove

one-legged Captain Ahab to steer the Pequod
in search of the white whale. She needs to know
Queequeg the harpooner and tattooed cannibal,
Starbuck the chief mate and Quaker from Nantucket,
and the meaning of Ishmael: "God listens."

ON THE BEACH IN ROTA, SPAIN

Celine, six, my granddaughter—*mi nieta*—
on this May evening, is steps ahead of me
looking for shells the waves brought in.

We wash the sand from them as waves come in.
She rushes her treasures to her Filipina mom
who walks behind with our first son, here in the Navy.

He was commissioned as an Ensign this week.
Our second son, here too, in the ceremony,
gave his brother the first salute. Celine runs ahead

giggling and calling out when she finds a shell. This is
all new to her. Granddad (Lolo) is old and seasoned.
The waves roll in and out as they have for millennia,

as they have for our thirty-three years of marriage. Here,
our first son, his wife and daughter, fit into the rhythm
of this cyclical life. They have many years ahead

to listen to the crash of waves, to step aside
from the rapidly moving bubbles and fizz. One day,
Celine will walk along a sandy beach

in a warm part of the world. No doubt,
a granddaughter will run to her and say
"Look, Lola, I found this pretty white one."

On the Beach in Rota, Spain

On the plane back to the States, I see Celine
on the sidewalk of Rota at *la feria*, her tiny fingers
clicking above her head of long black hair pulled up

and fitted with a rose. She dances her flamenco
in the flowing red and white ceremonial dress. She clicks
her fingers, taps her toes, and is at home in Andalusia.

UNITY

for Cat Pleska and the Martinez family

We are marvelously made—people, miracles
who fit no rigid, singular model. Look
at how our fingers work, how they can hold
another hand, help clear the blur in a friend's eye.
We can see without limit and count stars.

I see you, brother and sister. I hear your cries
and smell the smoke from the burning in your soul.
I hug you and feel the beat of your troubled heart.

For years, I've asked, at the Spanish Mass,
"Lord, I want to see your face." *Señor,*
quiero ver tu rostro. At the nativity celebration,

a line of two-year-old Hispanic girls entered
in white dresses with angel wings and walked
to the manger where Mary held her child.

One of the angels stopped, turned to the audience,
and danced to the guitars and song in Spanish
by the choir, *el coro.* She had every head turned.

Lord, I see your face. *Señor, veo tu rostro.*
Let me see you in everyone. Let me show the power
of love and forgiveness.

RED-WINGED BLACKBIRD

Here you are again, on the chain-link fence.
It's the same every day as I pass by
heading home—you perched there.
Are you waiting for someone?
Do you, like me, wonder what's next?

I'm often on the fence. Each day
I pray for success for my six children.
I can't rest until they're on their own,
thriving. My wife is the same.
We keep our eyes on hope.

Blackbird, you neither sow nor reap,
nor gather into barns. Do you question,
each day, how you will feed your family?

People urge me to write a will.
It's inevitable, but I feel responsible
and want to be here for them. I still talk
to my parents and am pretty sure they listen.

I don't know if you, blackbird, contemplate
these things each day like me.
I'll swing by again tomorrow.

TO THE TURDLES

Be careful if you have artistic tendencies
and you become a carpenter. You might prolong
framing jobs because you want perfection.
When the budget calls for "throw and go,"
and you are an aspiring Michelangelo,
your workmates might do what they did to me
when I took up carpentry again after being put out
to pasture by my corporate job.

I thought my young co-worker had called me
the T-word, but he later claimed he'd said "turtle"
to describe my slow pace. There were saws buzzing,
so he might have been truthful. After six weeks
on the job, I told the builder I do not fit
in a production environment.

It was a reminder of my years of self-employment
a century ago, when I had a carpentry business.
I know now why I never made a profit. It's tough
when you are on a fixed fee and trying to create
the Pietá for people, leveling and squaring cabinets
as if life depended on it.

Today, in homes, I see out-of-level door jambs,
shoddy tile jobs, tape peeling out in drywall. Oh,
look at that mismatched joint in the crown molding.
Get me out of here.

ROBIN NEST

Beneath a cypress tree, beside the driveway,
is a fallen nest—a five-inch diameter circle.
It's July, past when the babies trained to fly,
to find their place in this world. The mama

had no tape measure, no clippers, no pan
for mixing mud, yet she built this three-inch-tall
wrap of tiny twigs, interwoven and smoothed
with a mud coating pressed by her belly—

a soft spot for those lovely blue eggs. She sat
on them to keep them warm until the newborns
appeared with those long beaks outstretched.
The dad helped get the worms to feed them

for the couple of weeks it took for the hatchlings
to become brave enough to practice flight drills.
Off they went, eventually, gliding to the grass below,
to hop after insects and worms, these able bodies

from the Aves class. I watch the feeders carefully,
my eyes on the cat, my mind reviewing the love
in mamas, their ability to raise their wings and shriek
to protect their children. Ave, you mamas. *Ave Maria.*

DEATH ROW INTERVIEW

Leaves are falling. Our yard and driveway
display the cycle of oaks, hickories, maples,
sycamores, poplars, walnuts, and hackberries.

In an interview with a murderer, he said he'd been
on a Harley and shot the semi driver who'd gotten
too close. He then shot a trucker filling gas tanks.

The interviewer asked the guy about an afterlife.
He laughed and said, "We are bio mass, man. We are
like a leaf. It falls from a tree, and that's the end."

Surely he knows the complexity of leaves—how
they convert sunlight to chemical energy for food,
that food and water flow through veins of a leaf.

Leaves wave and show their many colors, their waxy
cuticles, the epidermis that protects from water loss,
and inside, the busy work that produces oxygen.

Now, they decompose to feed bacteria and critters
underground. Yes, it's hard to make sense of it—grow,
flourish, die, grow, flourish, die. I hear you, leaves.

SMELT ABOVE THE MOON

After four years in the Navy, I swore
never again to tolerate salty language.
Never would I allow four-letter words
to be used as seven parts of speech.

These are standard terms in the Navy.
I recall the alliteration of a Petty Officer
describing how a fellow sailor done him wrong:
"That F-ing mother F-er, he F-ing F-ed me over.
I am F-ing gonna F- up his F-ing face. S-!"

Behind me is that drill instructor and his greeting
at 4 AM in the barracks: "Alright, you S-birds,
drop your cocks and grab your socks. Pop tall.
It's time to s-, shower and shave."

I tell my children to be creative with language.
Though rhymes can be innovative, anyone
can use the B-word, the F-word, the A-word,
the S-word, and, God forbid, the C-word.
Making the common colorful takes imagination.

I explained to my teen, when he called me the B-word,
that I am male, not a female dog. Even son of a B-
would not be accurate as my Shakespeare-loving
British mother was classy and admirable.

Instead of being succinct and saying,
"Get the F- out of my room," he could say

"Please remove yourself to the far side of my threshold,
and pull the door gently closed as you depart."

Much can be said, though, about the visceral effects,
the satisfaction one derives from grinding out
those hard words, those elemental Anglo-Saxon sounds.
The F-word, S-word and a variety of C-word combinations
wrinkle the nose and force the face into a bark or snarl.

The language has suffered since *King Lear*
where Kent called Oswald "a knave; a rascal;
an eater of broken meats; a base, proud, shallow,
beggarly, three-suited, hundred-pound, filthy,
worsted-stocking knave; . . . one whom I will beat
into clamorous whining, if thou deniest
the least syllable of thy addition."

Hie thee hither. Yes, I have lapses, generally
out of earshot of my children and colleagues.
Like a vegetarian who occasionally slips
into the world of red meat for a taste, I indulge.
Be creative and colorful. Now get thee gone.

HIPPIE

"How beautiful are your feet in sandals,
O prince's daughter!
The curves of your hips are like jewels,
The work of the hands of an artist."

SONG OF SOLOMON 7:1
NEW AMERICAN STANDARD BIBLE

I was no hippie in the 1960s, my teen years.
My goal was to become a Catholic priest
until I discovered girls and whatever the force is
that drops men's jaws at the curves of women.

How can one think a woman is anything other than
the best of God's creations? With thirty-six years
of marriage, four daughters and three granddaughters,
I get it how blessed men are. There's no need to smack us,

ladies, to get our attention. We are already smitten.
I'm still trying to identify the pull, the endless draw
women have on us. And with the beauty, those curvy hips
bring forth the precious lives of children.

Thank you, ladies, for bringing us the highest art,
the miracle of life, and a glimpse of the divine.
As I drive home from work, on my left, the rolling hills
of the Blue Ridge are the hips of women.

TOILET PAPER

You'd think this private experience would never
cause fights. It's so normal. Yet, in this pandemic,
we've taken up arms against each other. My regular
shopping trips for four mega-packs have ended.
I live with six women: my wife, four daughters,
and a lovely granddaughter. We need TP.

In April, the cashier lady said I could only have
two of the four mega-packs. Behind me in line,
was a teacher for whom I had subbed. She said,
"Let me have the other two." Outside, I tried
to give $25 to her husband. They both refused
and gave me the mega-packs.

In May, I grabbed two mini-packs of TP and paid
via the self-checkout. As I bagged items, a lady said,
"You can only have one of them." "What? I've
already paid for them. I live with six women." I asked
for a manager. She arrived. "You can only have one
of them." "I've paid for them." "It is what it is, sir."

I picked up my two mini-packs and walked out.
They have me on camera, and my debit card is on file.
I expected to be stopped by the police. I got home
with no sirens. My wife called me a hero. I texted
a British cousin. She can't relate. They have bidets.
Back two days later, I wasn't thrown to the floor

or cuffed. No one bothered me. This time, I got one
mini-pack. I'm thinking of my British mother
who endured German bombs in England in WWII.
She raised us saying we should use only three sheets
of toilet paper. I never followed her instructions. I'll
shop every day if needed. Onward, TP warriors.

YES, THEY WERE HUNGRY

I still have pay stubs from McDonald's
where I worked in the 1960s in high school.
I made $1.10 per hour. We were allowed
to eat for free during breaks. We gobbled
burgers and fries. At Kentucky Fried Chicken,
we were able, at closing, to take home buckets
of extra cooked chicken. It was the way of life
in Northern Virginia.

When I got drafted and chose the Navy
in 1972 to avoid Vietnam, I was assigned
to ships that traveled around the world.
On one cruise, we circumnavigated Africa,
visited Iran, Pakistan, Bahrain, Sri Lanka,
and sailed through the Red Sea to the
Mediterranean. The first stop across the
Atlantic had been in Dakar, Senegal
along the northwestern coast of Africa.

It was the blank-eyed, homeless people
living in cardboard boxes on street corners
that woke me up. Barely clothed boys
surrounded us begging for help. We were
careful to protect our Kodak cameras and
wallets. I'd never heard of a famine before.

During many port stops, it was the same:
poor, homeless and hungry people were
everywhere in struggling countries. Today,

as I sit with my family and enjoy the
abundant dinners and view the full cabinets
of food at home, I take each bite with a prayer
of thanks.

FRANKENSTEINA

She's on the deck pouring potting soil
into containers. Without her careful,
persistent replenishing of plants each spring,
our yard would lack its beauty. She's made it
for fourteen years since the breast cancer.

She has Reflex Sympathetic Dystrophy (RSD)
in her swollen right hand. She'll possibly
overdo it and need to sleep for a couple of days.
The cancer meds have taken their toll:
hair and bone loss, sleep disorder, anxiety.

She's had meniscus surgery and has plans
for another operation for shoulder joint pain.
She adjusts her temporary front tooth.
We have six children. How could we
have made it without her?

She calls herself Frankensteina and notes
the new body parts: cadaver bones, screws
and plates from spinal surgery; a bilateral
silicone implant from breast surgery,
and hearing aids.

She's had cataract surgery on both eyes
and is hobbling on painful knee joints across
the deck tending to her tulips, daffodils
and irises. She pulls the hose behind her
and sprays life on the plants and all of us.

RAINBOW

for Joey

I'm working with an autistic student,
to follow a short article about rainbows.
We have five questions to answer. He has
little interest in following the answer key's
direction—the science about how rainbows
form and what atmospheric requirements
set the stage for them. He has his own answers.

Yes, you need the droplets of rain that fall
and the sun to shine on them to produce
the Newton spectrum of colors: red, orange,
yellow, green, blue, indigo and violet:
ROYBGIV. Many have disagreed about
the spectrum as far back as Aristotle, yet
we can all see the light, the semi-circle that
spreads across the sky after a storm.

I admire the first grader's determination,
but I made him check the answers provided
in the key. We have come a long way from
Noah's flood, but who knows all the facts?
Maybe he is on to something.

RUGGED FACE OF APPALACHIA

Oh Lord, when will the traffic stop?
I've been listening to the twang of tires
for way too long, and the exhaust noise
as vehicles climb the hill and pass by me.

There was a time when my limestone face
enjoyed the rising sun, the flocks of turkeys
hustling by, eagles and crows. But now, I feel
my chin coming loose. I've seen it before

from colleagues who share this wide expanse
of hillside beside the highway. They've lost
body parts. Below, along the road, are remnants
of ancestors. I guess we must accept that life

changes; we come and go despite being the
rugged foundation of these hills. Who would
have thought that minor breaks, over time,
could send us down? I just felt a crack.

SAMSON, OUR GREAT PYRENEES

For days, with a chainsaw, I cut up branches
that had fallen in our yard during the mini tornado.
There's your deep grave untouched by debris.
I am glad you weren't here to witness the chaos
and devastation. You would have howled
during the hail storm that beat down on our house
and cars. You also made it out of here before
the nights of fireworks on this 4th of July during
the pandemic. In your nearly eleven years,
you, big as a polar bear, hated fireworks.

I saw that look in your face the day before
we had to get the vet here to put you to rest.
You'd managed to hobble to your water bowl
a few times at the end. I saw a white laundry bag
behind the door the other day and thought
it was you. You talked to me on your last day
and knew you weren't able to move. Were you,
like me, asking for meaning as we whirl through
these COVID-19 times?

My wife, Beth, still weeps daily for you.
I'd done my job of digging your grave
in the back yard along the edge of the woods.
We miss you. We enjoyed all of those years
with you, Samson, trustworthy, strong, hairy
and able, if needed, to pull down pillars.

STATUE OF LIMITATIONS

It was in the early years of our marriage
when she said that. It didn't register
at first, but then I got it. I thought about
the Statue of Liberty with a copper hand
in front pushing away the immigrants
and pointing the torch toward them.
"Hold on," Libertas said. "There are limits."

I told my wife that she probably meant
"statute," not "statue." Many years have
passed since then. The statute has long
expired. We are so glad to be privileged
and free in America with our six children.
I attend a Spanish Mass *todos los domingos*
con mis amigos from Central and South
America. I welcome them to our rich land.

They work hard, support their families,
and continue to elevate their faith daily.
Yes, like my Irish ancestors who traveled
to Boston, I understand their journeys
and efforts to provide a new life for
their loved ones. This is America. We need
a multi-nation solution to this broken system.

Come, you huddled masses, let's find a
workable way to welcome you to America.
There is no statue of limitations.

COD FISHER

Alone in Gloucester my soft wife awaits me
while I, with crusted brow, must watch this squall
churn up the rippled wake with the salty sea.

My leathered fingers number months painfully
since boatswains cast us off, while on the sea wall
alone in Gloucester my soft wife awaits me.

I'm hawser-burned, hook-stabbed, and long to see
this wind-blown schooner's homeward rise and fall
churn up the rippled wake with the salty sea.

My father and his were borne by fishery,
and so am I, but wrapped in her woolen shawl,
alone in Gloucester, my soft wife awaits me.

The fantail winch, my creaking company,
lays out its coils that, in a taut-line trawl,
churn up the rippled wake with the salty sea.

This ship's as fish-filled as she cares to be.
Take hold your lines and give your nets their haul.
Alone in Gloucester, my soft wife awaits me.
Churn up the rippled wake with the salty sea.

PERFUME

The elevator was empty
when the doors opened on my floor.
I walked in, and the scent of perfume
lifted me. Who had she been, the one
who left springtime on the seventh floor
during late winter?

On my way to the deli, I was in love.
Outside, amid patches of snow,
crocuses and irises, aroused,
began to break through hard ground,
and the libidinous sap in the trees
was beginning to rise.

9 781666 766707